CONTEMPORARY PUBLIC OPINION
Issues and the News

COMMUNICATION TEXTBOOK SERIES

Jennings Bryant—Editor

Journalism
Maxwell McCombs—Advisor

CONTEMPORARY PUBLIC OPINION
Issues and the News

Maxwell McCombs
University of Texas at Austin

Edna Einsiedel
University of Calgary

David Weaver
Indiana University

IEA LAWRENCE ERLBAUM ASSOCIATES, PUBLISHERS
1991   Hillsdale, New Jersey   Hove and London

Lawrence Erlbaum Associates, Inc., Publishers
365 Broadway
Hillsdale, New Jersey 07642

Library of Congress Cataloging-in-Publication Data

McCombs, Maxwell E.
    Contemporary public opinion : issues and the news / Maxwell
McCombs, Edna Einsiedel, and David Weaver.
        p.   cm. – (Communication textbook series. Journalism)
    Includes bibliographical references and indexes.
    ISBN 0-8058-0537-0. – ISBN 0-8058-1102-8 (pbk.)
    1. Public opinion – United States. 2. Mass media – Social aspects –
United States. I. Einsiedel, Edna F. II. Weaver, David H. (David
Hugh), 1946-   . III. Title. IV. Series.
HN90.P8M43   1991
303.3 '8 '0973--dc20   91-16323
                                                                 CIP

Printed in the United States of America
10 9 8 7 6 5 4 3 2 1

Contents

Preface

In 1922 Walter Lippmann published his classic, *Public Opinion*. Except for the fact that his contemporary examples are now very dated—and in some instances so obscure that even the present authors have difficulty explaining them—it is a book that is still very much up to date in its discussion of the role of the news media in the formation of public opinion. When college students are not fully convinced by the elaboration of this argument, one of us (Maxwell McCombs) simply asks them to consider what the merits of the book must be in order to stay in print for over two thirds of a century.

Moreover, *Public Opinion* is a book that reads well, the product of a facile writer who was the dean of American journalism for at least four decades. Its journalistic origins, its concern with explicating the role of the news media in the creation of public opinion, and its pivotal position in the intellectual history of research on the agenda-setting role of the news media all combine to make *Public Opinion* a critical benchmark for the book that we have written.

Our goal, like Lippmann's, is to present a lively discussion of the public opinion process with particular attention to the contributions of the news media. Given the background of the authors, it is unnecessary to confess that it is a discussion heavily influenced by the agenda-setting perspective, the view that the news media define to a significant degree what are the major issues of the day. But our purpose here is not to proselytize for that view or to present a new theory of public opinion. Our purpose is to integrate a variety of contemporary scholarship into a coherent picture of public opinion for a general audience. As a collation, our book has another intellectual forebear, Robert Lane and David Sears' book also titled *Public Opinion*, which some 25 years ago brought together a rich mosaic of social science research. In one sense, our book follows the same strategy—creation of a mosaic. But in substance it is closer to Lippmann's *Public Opinion* with its emphasis on the news media. Lippmann is the intellectual grandfather; Lane and Sears, an older cousin.

Like both of those books, no extensive background in the scholarly, empirical research on public opinion and mass communication is assumed here. The goal of this book is to provide that background and to stimulate further inquiry. We see our audience as a combination of the general public and college students, both advanced undergraduates and beginning graduate students. The common thread among all is an interest in understanding public opinion.

Finally, our thanks to everyone who made this book possible, from supportive friends and colleagues at our universities to the numerous scholars whose work over the years has contributed the pieces of the mosaic assembled here. Very special thanks go to the Institute for Advanced Study at Indiana University—and to Henry Remak, its director, and Cleve Wilhoit, its associate director—where McCombs spent June of 1990 editing three sets of chapters into a single book. Like public opinion, a book is a collaborative activity.

Maxwell McCombs
Edna Einsiedel
David Weaver

PART ONE

Introduction

Communication and Public Opinion

Things are not what they once were. But then they never were! In the realm of public affairs, classical democratic theory assumes universal knowledge. To the extent that the public affairs to be guided by informed public opinion are local affairs, the assumption has some plausibility. Popular wisdom has it that in the small villages and towns of colonial America—and even the small communities that were the stereotypical portrait of the United States well into the current century—everyone knew the public business of the community, and even a great deal of the private affairs.

In a world of primarily local affairs, coupled with no more than a modicum of technical complexity and with widespread knowledge of community feelings and interests, it is reasonable to expect that community leadership and government actions will be in harmony with public opinion. After all, public opinion is concerned with that array of topics, interests, and behaviors where the concerns of many different individuals in a community are dependent on mutual action, cooperation or, at a minimum, tacit consent for the fulfillment of specific goals.

This classical view of grassroots democracy and leadership assumes that most, if not all, of the problems to be engaged by public opinion and its expression through government are obtrusive in nature. By an obtrusive problem we mean that the major outlines of the topic are well known—primarily through direct experience—to all members of the community. To some extent, classical expressions of democratic theory view the origins of issue obtrusiveness as inherent in each individual as if knowledge and

3

awareness came to be there by divine revelation. A more realistic view of the social psychology of public knowledge attributes these perceptions of public issues to direct experience.

In a small community one can have direct experience of many public topics. Peer review takes on a very specific meaning under circumstances where numerous citizens can, in the words of the lawyers, testify of their own personal knowledge. Even in our time there are obtrusive national issues. Ronald Reagan was elected president in 1980, in part, because of his persuasive arguments that he could deal with inflation, a problem then highly obtrusive to almost all Americans. Everyday experiences in the grocery stores, shopping malls, and on their jobs had informed voters in detail about the erosion of the dollar.

However, it is doubtful that a majority of the public questions of the day have ever been fully obtrusive to the general public. Even in the idealized and romanticized days of the 18th and 19th centuries, local obtrusive issues did not fully dominate the public agenda. Foreign affairs, which are the best example of an unobtrusive issue, received considerable attention from the colonial leadership of America. Benjamin Franklin, Thomas Jefferson, and many others in the political elite of the American colonies spent considerable time in France and other foreign locales in order to inform themselves and to influence the direction of events critical to the survival of the new republic. Even at home it is doubtful that anything approaching universal knowledge existed on most questions of the day.[1] Setting a goal of universal literacy was a step in that direction, but that step did not come until the United States of America was in its adolescence. In short, there never have been all that many truly obtrusive issues!

If the number of obtrusive issues to be dealt with by public opinion was limited even in the 18th and early 19th centuries, consider the change in the public agenda as the focus of government action shifted from the town hall and county courthouse to Washington. Once, as the Census Bureau has documented in its decennial portraits of America, the vast majority of us did reside in small communities or on farms. Even those who lived in cities resided in urban communities that were small by today's standard. Now the majority of Americans reside in urban areas, either the central cities or the considerable suburbs of our major metropolitan areas. Although the change in our physical environment has been considerable, the change in our psychological environment has been enormous. The issues that engage the minds of the attentive public now are far more likely to be national and international in scope than local.

---

[1]For an overview of the contemporary situation, see Neuman, W. R. (1986). *The paradox of mass politics: Knowledge and opinion in the American electorate*. Cambridge, MA: Harvard University Press.

A few years ago, there was considerable public concern and Congressional activity regarding President Reagan's sale of weapons to Iran and the apparent diversion of millions of dollars in profits from these sales to the Contras in Nicaragua. Here was an issue on the public agenda that was simultaneously national and international.

The initial impact on public opinion of these revelations about White House dealings with Iran and Nicaragua was significant. Poll questions about public satisfaction with the President's overall performance in office as well as specific queries about dealings with Iran and the Contras provided precise statistics on public concern and dismay.

This is a contemporary, historically fleeting, example of public opinion about an unobtrusive issue. By an unobtrusive issue we mean, of course, one that is not amenable to the direct experience of most Americans. Of course, the extensive television coverage of the Congressional hearings focused considerable public attention on Oliver North—remember him?— and the administration's dealings with Iran and the Contras, but that was still second-hand, mediated experience. Today, most of the issues on the public agenda, most of the issues around which public opinion is formed, are unobtrusive in nature.

Walter Lippmann eloquently summarized this point in his 1922 classic, *Public Opinion*:

> The world that we have to deal with politically is out of reach, out of sight, out of mind. It has to be explored, reported, and imagined. Man is no Aristotelian god contemplating all existence at one glance. (p. 29)[2]

A DIVISION OF LABOR

This observation by Lippmann also outlines the division of intellectual labor in the formation of public opinion about a largely remote, unobtrusive world. It is a division of labor between individual citizens and the news media, which Lippmann took up in the opening pages of *Public Opinion*. The first chapter in his book is titled, "The World Outside and the Pictures in Our Heads." It is Lippmann's thesis that the news media, primarily newspapers in his day, are the principal conduit between the world outside and the images we hold in our minds of that world. Lippmann was not the first to express that idea, nor the first to note the limitations of journalism in fulfilling this social function for a democracy. But he did it more eloquently and succinctly than most. Three verbs in the middle of the passage just quoted—"explored, reported, and imagined"—parsimoniously capture the

---

[2]Lippmann, W. (1922). *Public opinion*. New York: Macmillan.

roles of the news media and public that are elaborated in subsequent chapters of this book.

Democratic theory long has assigned the news media a major role in *exploring* the political happenings of the world, both those public events that are part of everyday government as well as those private events that governing officials often go to great lengths to conceal. But there is a great deal more to review here than the traditional roles of the news media as conveyors of public knowledge or as watchdogs over the excesses of government. Journalism is an institution in its own right, increasingly a professionalized one with its own peculiar practices, traditions, and values that determine what is reported and how it is reported.[3] This is not a statement, even indirectly, about traditional concerns over political bias. Rather it is a statement about journalism as a genre of communication, and how the characteristics of this genre shape the news media's daily exploration and reporting of the world.

Whereas *reporting* usually is considered the province of the news media, full consideration of the task of news reporting quickly will bring the realization that reporting—the transmission of information about the world outside—is a transaction between two partners, the news media and the public. The most accurate, complete, and beautifully presented news report is worthless if no one pays any attention. Part of the skill of the journalist, both individual reporters and their editors, is to capture and hold the attention of citizens who typically invest a half hour or less per day in the news.[4] Reporting as a communication act involves both the efforts of the journalist to explore and write the news *and* the efforts of individual citizens to pay sufficient attention to this news to acquire its principal information.

But the work of the citizen does not end there. The world outside has to be shaped into a picture in the mind. It needs to be *imagined*, rather than left as a clutter of stray facts gleaned from the daily news. At least that is necessary if public opinion is to be based on meaningful perspectives. Informed public opinion requires an active imagination.[5]

Although a complete social psychology of public opinion would accord equal treatment to the partners in these daily transactions, citizens, and the news media, the tilt here is toward the news media and citizens' use of these sources. This is not to say that other aspects of political psychology are ignored. It simply is to say that citizen interaction with the news media and crucial aspects of the news media that influence the nature of public opinion

---

[3]See, for example, Golding, P., & Elliott, P. (1979). *Making the news*. London: Longman; and Sigal, L. (1973). *Reporters and officials: The organization and politics of newsmaking*. Lexington, MA: D.C. Heath.

[4]Bogart, L. (1989). *Press and public* (2nd ed.). Hillsdale, NJ: Lawrence Erlbaum Associates.

[5]Graber, D. (1988). *Processing the news* (2nd ed.). New York: Longman.

are emphasized. Otherwise, this book would run considerably longer than it does, and, at least for many readers, be far too encyclopedic in tone.

MEDIA INFLUENCE

· Reference was made earlier to the question of political bias in the news. Of all the popular questions involving political communication and public opinion, this is by far the dominant one. But on balance, there is little evidence over the past 40 years of any systematic partisan bias in the major television and newspaper coverage of campaigns.[6] In recent years, attention has shifted away from partisan bias and direct media influence on people's attitudes and opinions. There is far less concern with partisan bias in news coverage or direct persuasive influence by editorial and opinion pages in the newspaper. This is not to say that newspapers do not influence their readers, or that newspapers' editorial endorsements have no influence on the outcome of elections. They do! But the once massive influences ascribed to the news media, influences enshrined in such labels as the "bullet theory" or "hypodermic theory" of mass communication, have been replaced with more moderate views of mass media impact. One of these newer perspectives, which guides this discussion of public opinion, is the agenda-setting role of mass communication.[7] The difference between this view and other, older views of powerful media effects is summed up in political scientist Bernard Cohen's remark that the media may not tell us what to think, but they tell us what to think *about*.[8]

Through their day-by-day selection of news stories and decisions about how to display those stories, the editors of our newspapers and the producers of our local and national television news programs provide us with significant cues about what are the important issues of the day. This agenda-setting influence of the news media results from the necessity to choose some topics for the daily news report and to reject others, to select some stories for prominent headlines, display on the front page or the lead of a newscast, and to bury others deep in the news report. In any event, issues prominent on the news agenda are perceived by the public to be important, and, over time, frequently become the priority issues on the public agenda.

This agenda-setting influence results from what an early student of mass

---

[6]McCombs, M. (1972). Mass communication in political campaigns: Information, gratification and persuasion: In F. G. Kline & P. J. Tichenor (Eds.), *Current perspectives in mass communication research* (pp. 169–194). Beverly Hills: Sage.

[7]Protess, D., & McCombs, M. (Eds.). (1991). *Agenda-setting: Readings on media, public opinion and policymaking.* Hillsdale, NJ: Lawrence Erlbaum Associates.

[8]Cohen, B. (1963). *The press and foreign policy.* Princeton: Princeton University Press.

communication, sociologist and former journalist Robert Park, called the "signal function" of the news. Stories and reports in the news signal the public that the life of an individual or some situation involving a number of individuals has departed from normal paths of behavior.[9] Usually the measure of departure from the normal is the fact that some aspect of this situation has entered the jurisdiction of a government or public institution. There has been an arrest or indictment, a law suit has been filed or decided, a regulation or law has been promulgated. These specific acts, circumscribed events that can be described in summary form by journalists, signal that something has changed in the world. But in order to be reported by the news media, these events also must be intrinsically interesting in their own right and/or involve the interests of enough people or groups to make them socially significant.

The mundane—at least to most members of the public—world of city planning and zoning illustrates these criteria. If Barbara Smith applies to the city government for a building permit to construct a swimming pool in her backyard, it is a matter of concern to only a few neighbors at most. Or if her husband, Sam Smith, applies for a variance in the zoning regulations to expand his furniture store located along one of the major streets of the city, again it is of little concern to most people. The news media are unlikely to take notice of either application. But if the state university seeks building permits for a residential and commercial development on 200 acres of vacant land that it owns adjacent to a large recreational lake and several of the city's most expensive neighborhoods, the interests of numerous groups and individuals are engaged. And the news media will take notice!

Even though two aspects of the Smiths' life move into official government channels, there is nothing that journalists would consider newsworthy. Neither of these matters are public affairs or the focus of public opinion as these terms are used here. But the university's development plans clearly are both. Continued attention to these plans by the local newspapers and television stations also will suggest to most of the public that this is a public issue of considerable importance.[10] News coverage will stimulate the rise of this issue on the public agenda of the community. Public opinion will form and exert, in turn, its influence on the history and subsequent news coverage of this issue.

In considering this agenda-setting role of the news media, it is important

---

[9]Shoemaker, P., Chang, T., & Brendlinger, N. (1987). Deviance as a predictor of newsworthiness: Coverage of international events in the U.S. media: In M. L. Laughlin (Ed.), *Communication yearbook 10* (pp. 348–365). Newbury Park, CA: Sage.

Shoemaker, P. (1987). The communication of deviance: In B. Dervin & M. J. Voight (Eds.), *Progress in communication sciences* (Vol 8, pp. 151–175). Norwood, NJ: Ablex.

[10]Downs, A. (1972). Up and down with ecology—The "issue attention" cycle. *Public Interest, 12*, 38–50.

to note that the influence of newspapers and broadcasters is limited primarily to influencing the *salience* of an issue. The play of an issue on the news agenda influences the perceived prominence of an issue. The play of an issue does not necessarily influence the distribution of opinions on an issue. But it can![11] Continuing the example just used, prominent coverage of the university's development plans almost certainly will move that topic onto the public agenda. But even if this coverage is one-sided, heavily negative, or favorably propagandistic, reaction by the public may have little correlation. It may tilt in the direction suggested by the news coverage, move in the opposite direction, or it may be evenly divided between those in favor and those opposed. The agenda-setting role of the news media focuses on the salience of opinions, not their direction.

In this sense, the news media are the parents of public opinion on many issues. They give birth to issues, and they have some influence on the direction of their offspring. But public issues, like children, grow up and live out their lives in considerable independence of their parents. For some issues, of course, especially at the local level, the news media do not even have the role of mother and father. For truly obtrusive issues, those where members of the public have direct personal experience, the news media are relegated to minor, sometimes nonexistent, roles in the formation of public opinion.

SURVEILLANCE AND LEADERSHIP

Daily surveillance of the world outside is the principal function of journalism. To understand the relationship between the daily report resulting from this surveillance and the collective set of pictures in our heads that are the portrait of public opinion, it is necessary to understand the standards and procedures that go into the construction of the daily news report and to understand how members of the public incorporate this report into their pictures of the world. The surveillance function of the news media is an important social contribution. On those occasions that this surveillance also contributes to the achievement of consensus in a community or across the nation, the agenda-setting role of the news media also is an important component of its leadership function.

In the formation of public opinion both the news media and the public

---

[11]But increasingly there is evidence that it can! See, for example, Page, B., Shapiro, R., & Dempsey, G. (1989). What moves public opinion? *American Political Science Review, 81,* 23–43.

Fan, D., & Tims, A. (1989). The impact of the news media on public opinion: American presidential election 1987–1988. *International Journal of Public Opinion Research, 1,* 151–163.

have surveillance and leadership roles to perform. As Lippmann remarked, the world outside must be explored, reported, and imagined.

In all of this, press and public are constrained by the limitations of communication, constraints that limit the ability of both individual and mass communicators to construct comprehensive portraits of the day's events or to merge these snapshots into a coherent view of the world outside. Public opinion is based on a fragmentary, often incomplete and distorted, set of pictures. After all, Walter Lippmann consciously prefaced *Public Opinion* with Plato's allegory of the cave where the prisoners in the cave could see only the reflections of reality on the wall before them.

CHAPTER TWO

The Agenda-Setting Role
of Mass Communication

Democratic theory assumes more than knowledge of and participation in government affairs by numerous citizens and groups. Democratic theory also assumes some agreement on what the most important issues of the day are. In fact, any system of government can deal with only a limited set of issues or problems in a given time period.[1] There must be not only a finite set of issues, but also a sense of the priority, or ranking, of these issues that defines an agenda to which governmental institutions can respond by authoritatively allocating resources.

Such an agenda does more than make possible an organized system of allocating resources. It also contributes to notions of community and nationality. Knowledge of what the important issues are, and a stake in their resolution, forms the basis for discussion and participation in a larger community.

Because many citizens of a country as large and complex as ours are not directly involved with government or with groups concerned about particular issues, they must rely on other sources of information for their ideas about which issues are more or less important—the agendas of national, state, and even local governments. The most available and frequent sources of such information include newspapers, radio, television, and news magazines—the mass media. These sources, especially newspapers, have been

---

[1]Easton, D. (1965). *A systems analysis of political life*. New York: Wiley; and Easton, D. (1965). *A framework for political analysis*. Englewood Cliffs, NJ: Prentice-Hall.

found in numerous studies during the past two decades to play an important role in setting the public agenda.[2]

But this role is neither ubiquitous nor all-powerful. The mass media by themselves do not simply dictate what the public agenda will be for all citizens, independent of what influential news sources think or what motives and interests that individual citizens have. The process is considerably more complex and variegated than the simple phrase "media agenda setting" might seem to imply. As Walter Lippmann put it:

> For it is clear enough that under certain conditions men respond as powerfully to fictions as they do to realities, and that in many cases they help to create the very fictions to which they respond. (p. 14)[3]

In other words, people are not passive receivers of the news media or other messages. People actively construct their pictures of reality, but they are constrained by the information available to them from the mass media and other sources. This chapter describes briefly what we know about media agenda setting after nearly two decades of systematic research and many more decades of impressionistic, often insightful, observation. It also links what we know about media agenda setting to the formation of public opinion on issues of the day.

WHAT IS MEDIA AGENDA SETTING?

The notion of agenda setting has its roots in Lippmann's idea of "the pictures in our heads" and in Bernard Cohen's more recent observation in *The Press and Foreign Policy* that "the press may not be successful much of the time in telling people what to think, but it is stunningly successful in telling its readers what to think about" (p. 13).[4] In other words, even though the media may not be very successful at telling us what opinions to hold, they are often quite influential in telling us what to have opinions about.

---

[2]See, for example, McCombs, M. E., & Shaw, D. L. (1972). The agenda-setting function of mass media. *Public Opinion Quarterly, 36,* 176–187.

Shaw, D. L., & McCombs, M. E. (1977). *The emergence of American political issues: The agenda-setting function of the press.* St. Paul, MN: West.

Weaver, D. H., Graber, D. H., McCombs, M. E., & Eyal, C. H. (1981). *Media agenda-setting in a presidential election: Issues, images, and interest.* New York: Praeger.

MacKuen, M. B., & Coombs, S. L. (1981). *More than news: Media power in public affairs.* Newbury Park, CA: Sage.

Iyengar, S., & Kinder, D. R. (1987). *News that matters: Television and American opinion.* Chicago: University of Chicago Press.

[3]Lippman, W. (1922). *Public opinion.* New York: Macmillan.

[4]Cohen, B. (1963). *The press and foreign policy.* Princeton: Princeton University Press.

In this rather simple observation, Cohen made an important distinction between what we think about (cognitions) and what we think (opinions or feelings). This distinction has been important to psychologists for years, who have studied not only cognitions and opinions, but also behavior—and the links between thoughts, feelings, and behavior. But to many observers of mass media effects, it was an intellectual breakthrough to be reminded that the media can have strong cognitive effects without necessarily having strong direct effects on opinions and behavior.

This was especially true after almost 30 years of social science evidence demonstrating the limited ability of mass media messages to change political attitudes or candidate preferences.[5] In 1960, Joseph Klapper concisely summarized the general finding of much of this earlier research in his often quoted conclusion that "Mass communication *ordinarily* does not serve as a necessary and sufficient cause of audience effects, but rather functions among and through a nexus of mediating functions and influences" (p. 8).[6]

Although Klapper's conclusion was comforting to those in the media who sought to disclaim any responsibility for possible harmful effects of violent programs, incomplete news reporting, misleading advertising, and so forth, it did not satisfy those who believed that mass media were important influences on public opinion and the pictures in our heads that Lippmann wrote about nearly 40 years earlier.

There certainly were findings from those early election studies that suggested voters do indeed learn about politics from the mass media, even if very few changed their opinions in the short run of campaigns. For example, the 1948 Elmira election study found that those with the most exposure to the mass media were most likely to know where the candidates stood on different issues.[7] Even the person with little interest in politics inadvertently acquired some political information, although this information did not lead immediately to opinion change because political opinions typically are built up slowly over time.

Against the backdrop of these earlier findings on learning, Maxwell McCombs and Donald Shaw[8] explored the idea of agenda setting during the 1968 presidential election. Comparing the rankings of issues by newspapers and television with the rankings of those same issues by undecided voters, they found evidence that the amount of coverage and emphasis on certain

---

[5]See, for example, Lazarsfeld, P., Berelson, B., & Gaudet, H. (1948). *The people's choice.* New York: Columbia University Press; Berelson, B., Lazarsfeld, P., & McPhee, W. (1954). *Voting.* Chicago: University of Chicago Press; Katz, E., & Lazarsfeld, P. (1955). *Personal influence.* New York: The Free Press; and Trenaman, J., & McQuail, D. (1961). *Television and the political image.* London: Methuen.

[6]Klapper, J. (1960). *The effects of mass communication.* New York: The Free Press.

[7]Berelson, Lazarsfeld, & McPhee, op. cit.

[8]McCombs & Shaw, op. cit.

issues by the news media had a strong effect on (or, at least, a strong correlation with) which issues these voters considered most and least important in the 1968 election. They also found that even though the three presidential candidates (Nixon, Humphrey, and Wallace) placed widely different emphasis upon those issues, the voters' agenda reflected the overall agenda of the news media rather than any particular candidate's agenda.

McCombs and Shaw interpreted these findings as suggesting that mass media may have little direct effect on political opinions and attitudes, but that they have a significant cumulative effect on cognitions—the agenda of issues that voters have opinions about.

At last there was empirical evidence to suggest that the media might have important effects, something that many scholars, politicians, advertisers and others had suspected intuitively for decades. And this agenda-setting effect seemed to override selective exposure, perception, and retention—forces that contribute to *reinforcement* rather than *change* of attitudes and opinions in earlier studies of media effects.

Even though this benchmark agenda-setting study by McCombs and Shaw was a reassertion of powerful media effects, it was not an assertion of universal, undifferentiated effects on all voters. Individual differences in the judgments of the voters about the important issues of the day were lost by lumping all of them together in an aggregate portrait of the public agenda. In terms of specific findings, the correlations between news media and voter agendas in this initial study of agenda-setting were not uniform across all the media and all groups of voters.

The strength of support for the idea of media agenda setting varies according to which kind of portrait of public opinion is under scrutiny.[9] Portraits based in aggregate public data, such as the results of public opinion polls, and a broad set of issues generally find that the relative media emphasis on these issues influences the relative size of groups in the community who are most concerned about these same issues. This is especially true for unobtrusive issues, those that are least likely to be directly experienced by citizens, such as foreign politics, military expenditures, and so on. These aggregate pictures of public opinion do not mean that each person's agenda is identical to the media agenda, but this is still an important public effect of mass communication with distinct political implications, given the closeness of many U.S. elections.

In a year-long study of the 1976 U.S. presidential election, the influence of both newspapers and television on this broad pattern of public concern over issues was greatest during the spring and summer and least during the

---

[9]For more details on these points, including references to specific studies, see Weaver, D. (1984). Media agenda-setting and public opinion: Is there a link? In R. N. Bostrom & B. H. Westley (Eds.), *Communication yearbook 8* (pp. 680–691). Newbury Park, CA: Sage.

final few months of the campaign, especially for the unobtrusive issues of foreign affairs, government credibility, and the environment.[10] Distinctions between newspapers and television as issue agenda setters also became less pronounced as the campaign progressed. The newspaper agenda remained quite stable over time, whereas the television agenda became more similar to the newspapers'.

In contrast to the declining importance of newspapers and television as agenda setters later in the year, the motives of voters became more important as the campaign drew to a close. Those voters who were most uncertain about whom to support, and at the same time most interested in the election, had issue agendas in the last few months of the campaign that were substantially more similar to the media agendas than did other voters.

But when the comparison is more narrowly drawn between a set of issues and an individual's personal agenda, there is considerably less support for media agenda setting.[11] In a way, this is not surprising. Few would expect the exact ranking of a set of issues by the news media to be reflected in the rankings of these same issues by each individual person. If this were the case, we would be back to a "hypodermic needle" or "magic bullet" theory of media effects, where media messages are injected or shot directly into individual persons.

We know things are more complicated and less mechanical than that. The same media messages do not have exactly the same effects on all people, and all important public effects of the media cannot be measured solely in terms of individual persons. It is frequently necessary to consider media impact on groups of persons or on society as a whole.

OTHER PORTRAITS

When portraits of public opinion use aggregate poll data to measure the rise and fall of public concern about a single issue, rather than an entire set of issues, there is considerable support for the notion of media agenda-setting. Political scientist Michael MacKuen compared Gallup public opinion data and measures of media agendas from three national news magazines (*Time, Newsweek,* and *U.S. News & World Report*) from 1960 to 1977, as well as "real-world" measures of unemployment, inflation, crime rates, heating fuel prices, and troop levels in South Vietnam. He concluded:

---

[10]Weaver, Graber, McCombs, & Eyal, op. cit.

[11]See, for example, McLeod, J. M., Becker, L. B., & Byrnes, J. E. (1974). Another look at the agenda-setting function of the press. *Communication research, 1,* 131–165.

Weaver, D. H., Stehle, T. E., Auh, T. S., & Wilhoit, G. C. (1975). *A path analysis of individual agenda-setting during the 1974 Indiana senatorial campaign.* Paper presented at the Association for Education in Journalism, Ottawa, Canada.

the shape of citizen agendas clearly reflects the editorial judgments defining news coverage, but is also sensitive to the real world . . . independent of the media's orientations. (p. 141)[12]

Although the *character* of events, how dramatic they are, is ultimately more important than the *amount* of news coverage in accounting for media impact on public agendas, the relationship between amount of coverage and public concern "stands strong and there seems little doubt that such a correspondence exists" (p. 22).[13]

In a more recently published local study that compared 22 public opinion surveys in Louisville, Kentucky, with measures of the *Louisville Times* newspaper agendas from 1974 to 1981, Kim Smith found that public concern and newspaper coverage seemed to mutually influence each other for some issues (education, economic development, and crime), that newspaper coverage influenced public concern for some issues (environment and local government), and that public concern influenced newspaper coverage of other issues (public recreation and health care).[14]

Finally, those portraits of public opinion that analyze issues one-by-one and look for individual differences that reflect exposure to the news offer differing levels of support for media agenda setting, depending on the design of the research. The weakest design, a survey at one point in time, yields the weakest support, but even this evidence of media influence is no weaker than that provided by measures of real-world conditions or individual characteristics.[15]

More recent field experiments produce considerably stronger support for the agenda-setting effects of the news media upon individuals. Northwestern University researchers found a "clear agenda-setting effect" of an NBC televised investigative news report on fraud in federally funded home health care.[16] Using a before–after experimental design with 300 randomly selected members of the Chicago public who were asked to watch either of two TV programs airing at the same time, the authors found a substantial increase in concern over the health-care issue among members of the group that watched the program, but not among those who did not watch it. They also found an increase in concern among government officials who viewed the program, and more willingness to advocate action to correct the problem.

---

[12]MacKuen & Coombs, op. cit., p. 141.

[13]Ibid., 22.

[14]Smith, K. (1987). Newspaper coverage and public concern about community issues. *Journalism Monographs, 101.*

[15]Erbring, L., Goldenberg, E., & Miller, A. (1980). Front-page news and real-world cues: A new look at agenda-setting by the media. *American Journal of Political Science, 24,* 16–49.

[16]Cook, F., Tyler, T., Goetz, E., Gordon, M., Protess, D., Leff, D., & Molotch, H. (1983). Media and agenda-setting: Effects on the public, interest group leaders, policy makers, and policy. *Public Opinion Quarterly, 47,* 16–35.

Another set of experiments at Yale University found evidence that "strongly supports" media agenda setting. Researchers there altered TV newscasts for 6 days by substituting previously videotaped stories on several issues in order to increase TV news attention to them.[17] They found increases in individual concern for two of the problems emphasized in the newscasts (defense shortcomings and pollution from energy generation), but not for the third (inflation), probably because concern over inflation was already very high and because it is a more obtrusive issue that has a direct impact on everyone.

Taken together, these portraits of public opinion suggest that sustained emphasis by the news media on certain issues (especially those with which most people have little direct experience) is likely to result in public concern over those issues, but the precise ranking of a set of issues by the media is not likely to be reflected in the rankings of those issues by each individual person. But it also is clear that public concern over some issues can precede media emphasis on those issues. In the formation of public agendas, the media do not always lead.

As Walter Lippmann put it so well:

Unless the event is capable of being named, measured, given shape, made specific, it either fails to take on the character of news, or it is subject to the accidents and prejudices of observation. . . . the quality of the news about modern society is an index of its social organization. The better the institutions, the more all interests concerned are formally represented, the more issues are disentangled . . . (p. 363)[18]

The public agenda is also set by other institutions and groups besides the media, but the media seem to have taken on added importance as agenda setters in the 1970s and 1980s with the decline in the influence of political parties and increased emphasis on the polling of individuals.

CONSEQUENCES OF AGENDA SETTING

What difference does it make to public opinion if some issues are regarded as more important than others? If the media are important in elevating the salience, or prominence, of some issues over others, what are the implications for public opinion, elections, and public policy?

---

[17]Iyengar, S., Peters, M., & Kinder, D. (1982). Experimental demonstrations of the 'not-so-minimal' consequences of television news programs. *American Political Science Review, 76,* 848–858.

[18]Lippmann, op. cit., p. 363.

It is one thing to demonstrate that media emphasis on certain issues (and neglect of others) has an effect on how important these issues are considered by the public, but it is quite another thing to demonstrate that the perceived salience of an issue matters in terms of public opinion, behavior, and policy.

In recent years, however, the links between agenda setting and public opinion have received close scrutiny. In general, stronger links exist between increased salience and knowledge about an issue than between increased salience and opinions on that issue. This is not surprising, considering that information gain is not always correlated with opinion change. Different people can interpret the same information in different ways.

Sometimes increased attention by the news media, and subsequent increased public concern, is associated with more favorable public opinion and sometimes with more negative opinion. For example, one study found that the sheer amount of exposure to the news media was the strongest predictor of the public's support for Congress. Use of media was a stronger predictor of public support for Congress than political party affiliation, political participation, sense of political effectiveness, and a number of other factors. "Perhaps it is not the content of the media messages, but simply the fact of extensive coverage that elevates the standing of governmental institutions" (p. 610).[19]

On the other hand, a comparison of public opinion polls and magazine coverage on fluoridation and nuclear power from 1950 to 1975 found a correlation between amount of media coverage of these issues and public reaction against them, suggesting that the increased salience of those topics resulted in *negative* public opinion. The author suggested that "media coverage of scientific controversies may do more than define and amplify an event; it may have profound effects on public attitudes, the precise nature of which is difficult to specify" (p. 109).[20]

Another example of increased issue salience resulting in negative public opinion was documented in a 7-year study in Louisville, Kentucky, that found amount of newspaper coverage of various issues correlated over time with both higher levels of public concern over these issues and more negative evaluations of government services.[21] Given such findings, it is little wonder that some scientists and government officials shun media coverage of their activities!

There are other examples of a significant correlation between the salience

---

[19]Davidson, R., & Parker, G. (1972). Positive support for political institutions: The case of Congress: *Western Politics Quarterly, 25,* 600–610.

[20]Mazur, A. (1981). Media coverage and public opinion on scientific controversies. *Journal of Communication, 31,* 106–115.

[21]Smith, K. A. (1987). Effects of newspaper coverage on community issue concerns and local government evaluations. *Communication Research, 14,* 379–395.

of issues and public opinion. A 1972 election survey in Madison, Wisconsin, found that those voters who considered honesty in government and the Vietnam war more important than crime and world leadership were less likely to prefer Richard Nixon over George McGovern for president.[22]

The strongest evidence to date for a direct link between agenda setting and the movement of public opinion is found in an extensive analysis of 80 public policy issues during the past two decades. Nearly half the aggregate changes in preferences were accounted for by network television coverage.[23]

More recent experiments with television news also have found that "The media's agenda does seem to alter the standards people use in evaluating the president" (p. 853).[24] For the subjects in this experiment, defense performance was powerful in determining their ratings of President Jimmy Carter after a week's worth of TV news stories emphasizing U.S. defense capabilities.

This outcome is the result of a psychological process called *priming*, whereby media emphasis on particular issues not only confers status (or increases salience), but also activates in people's memories previously acquired information about these issues. That information is then used in forming opinions about persons, groups, or institutions linked to these issues.

Further evidence that agenda setting is linked to public opinion, knowledge, and behavior is provided from a 1988 Indiana statewide survey of 746 randomly selected respondents that asked people how concerned they were about the issue of the federal budget deficit, as well as their opinions about this issue, their knowledge of possible causes and solutions, and their behavior.[25] The more concerned people were about the federal budget deficit, the more they knew about it, the stronger their opinions, and the more likely they were to take some action about it, such as writing letters, signing petitions, attending meetings, or voting a certain way. Those who were most concerned also were more likely to favor cuts in spending on social programs and least likely to be neutral about spending cuts. But there was no correlation between the perceived importance of the federal budget deficit and opposing spending cuts, illustrating once again how difficult it is to predict the *direction* of public opinion on an issue just from its salience.

It is likely that increased salience of an issue will result in more public knowledge and stronger public opinions, but it is less certain what direction that opinion will take. Direction of opinion depends not only on what past

---

[22]Becker, L. B., & McLeod, J. M. (1976). Political consequences of agenda-setting. *Mass Comm Review, 3,* 8–15.

[23]Page, B. T., Shapiro, R. Y., & Dempsey, G. R. (1987). What moves public opinion?. *American Political Science Review, 81,* 23–43.

[24]Iyengar, Peters, & Kinder, op. cit, p. 853.

[25]Weaver, D. (1991). Issue salience and public opinion: Are there consequences of agenda-setting? *International Journal of Public Opinion Research, 3,* 53–68.

beliefs and values each person brings to media messages, but also on how issues are presented by the media in terms of group interests and values, as well as perspectives that are developed through discussion with other persons.

> Differences of opinion may actually reflect fundamental differences in beliefs about the issue itself. Is nuclear power an economic issue or a safety issue? Opposing sides in a public dispute may construe it in quite different ways. (p. 792)[26]

There is also evidence that media emphasis on certain issues may influence not only public opinion, but also government officials' agendas and opinions. The previously mentioned field experiment in Chicago found that an investigative news report on the federally funded home health-care program had significant effects on the agendas of both the public and policymakers. It also found policy changes as a result of this broadcast.[27]

A May 1984 television series on the storing of toxic chemical and radioactive wastes at the University of Chicago had limited effects on the general public, but did change the views of policymakers as to the importance of the issue and led to inspections and citations by the Chicago Fire Department.[28]

These news reports are most likely to have effects on opinions when they provide unambiguous presentations of nonrecurring issues—such as reports on fraud and abuse in home health care. But media effects are likely to be weaker when the issues are recurring and commonly covered and when the reports are more ambiguous—such as whether storing of certain toxic wastes violates government regulations.[29]

CONCLUSIONS

It should be clear by now that agenda setting is a complex process that involves not only the news media, but also other institutions and groups. Nevertheless, we can no longer assume that the media mainly reinforce

---

[26]Price, V., & Roberts, D. F. (1987). Public opinion processes. In C. R. Berger & S. H. Chaffee (Eds.), *Handbook of communication science* (pp. 781–816). Newbury Park, CA: Sage.

See also Price, V. (1988). On the public aspects of opinion *Communication Research, 15*, 659–679, for a discussion of the importance of group memberships and discussion with others in the formation of public opinion.

[27]Cook et al., op. cit.

[28]Protess, D. L., Cook, F. L., Curtin, T. R., Gordon, M. T., Leff, D. R., McCombs, M. E., & Miller, P. (1987). The impact of investigative reporting on public opinion and policymaking. *Public Opinion Quarterly, 51*, 166–185.

[29]Ibid.

preexisting opinions and attitudes, as the studies from the 1940s and 1950s seemed to show. Mass communication is an important influence in the formation and change of public opinion, mainly through its ability to raise the salience of certain issues and certain aspects of those issues, as well as the salience of positions taken by different groups and individuals.

PART TWO

Exploring the News

CHAPTER THREE

Practices, Values, and Traditions in Journalism

The news that we see and read each day is a manufactured commodity. But unlike nearly all the other commodities that we consume, each news item is a newly crafted cultural commodity. And unlike standardized consumer goods, news items reflect the creativity and idiosyncrasies of both the reporter who originated the item and the editors who guided it through the news organization as well as the traditions of a profession that has evolved through the daily production of news items in the United States for the past 150 years.[1]

In one sense, of course, news items are standardized commodities moving in commercial channels. Increasingly, journalism schools in our colleges and universities standardize the professional education of journalists. As newsrooms become part of larger and larger bureaucracies, organizational imperatives exert a greater degree of standardization on what we actually read and see. Now all of this is true to some degree for many other professions and many other commodities. What makes journalism different is that its inventory of items on any day ranges from a dozen or so to several hundred, and this inventory is completely refurbished every 24 hours. This rapid turnover in inventory and the need to constantly create new commodities introduces the idiosyncrasies of the individual journalist into the midst of a highly routinized and bureaucratized profession. In short, a number of factors combine to influence how the daily news is reported.

---

[1]Reese, S., & Shoemaker, P. (1991). *Mediating the message: Theories of influence on mass media content*. New York: Longman.

To gain an overview of these influences, that venerable metaphor, peeling the onion, is a useful device. In this chapter we examine a journalistic onion composed of three layers of influence. Starting at the outside, these layers are the practices and policies of news organizations, the values and individual differences of journalists, and the traditions of journalism as a genre of mass communication. Each of these levels of analysis, each of these perspectives on journalistic behavior, incorporates and modifies all the influences and factors on the inner levels of the onion. Put another way, the third, inner-most level represents the core of journalistic traditions, practices, and values. But the direction supplied by these traditions, practices, and values is further specified by other layers of influence as the daily news takes shape.

NEWS ORGANIZATIONS

We begin to peel the onion with an examination of how news organizations impact the daily news report. This outermost layer of influence on the daily news is sociological, growing out of the character and style of news organizations themselves. Formal organizations—in our case, individual newspapers, magazines, and television networks—have distinct personalities and styles. *The New York Times* and the *Washington Post* have vastly different communication styles that are perceptible to even the most casual reader. As organizations, they also have very different styles.[2] It has been observed that *The New York Times* is an editor's paper, whereas the *Post* is a reporter's paper. At the *Post* most reporters work in the newsroom and have direct access to the editors. Conversely, editors feel considerable pressure to deal face-to-face with reporters about any objections they have in regard to the way a story is written. In contrast, the geographic dispersion of the *Times* reporters—a large Washington staff, plus bureaus in numerous American cities and foreign capitals—leaves considerable power over news copy in the hands of the New York editors. It would take only a short visit to the newsrooms of these two major dailies to feel the difference. Embedded in these differences are variations in policy and approaches to the news.

Beyond these idiosyncratic differences in the practice of journalism from newspaper to newspaper and network to network, there also are organizational influences that are common across organizations. ABC and CBS may have different corporate personalities; nevertheless, they share many corporate traits by virtue of being large news organizations headquartered in New York who are in the business of producing daily television news.

Edward Jay Epstein's *News from Nowhere* is a classic exposition of how organizational constraints shape the daily network news report.

---

[2]Sigal, L. (1973). *Reporters and officials*. Lexington, MA: D. C. Heath.

News is essentially protean in character. Any happening can be reported in a multitude of different forms and takes on radically different appearances in different news media. Nor is there necessarily one correct way of reporting an event. Alternative ways exist for organizing information, and events themselves do not ineluctably determine the forms in which they are reported. Yet in examining the product of a news organization, one may find striking similarities in the ways in which the news is presented and the direction it takes. (p. 259)[3]

Foremost among these constraints is the organizational necessity to present a daily news report within the boundaries of a monetary budget. Although all news organizations must live with budgetary constraints, the particularly high costs of news stories for a national television report makes this consideration especially imperative for the networks.

Among the key implications of this budgetary constraint documented by Epstein are:

- A limited number of camera crews assigned to no more than a dozen or so news stories each day. This underscores the need for predictable stories—events that will play out on schedule and fit typical story lines.
- A restricted geography with major emphasis on New York and Washington. This keeps the transmission costs for stories to a minimum. When stories are used from other locales, priority generally goes to that handful of major cities where the networks own affiliates (and thus have permanent communication links) or where commercial competition keeps the long distance transmission charges down.
- A small group of news makers—mostly high status individuals—engaged in conflict or seeking major political office. This also maximizes the likelihood of usable stories.

Each of these practices is an outcome of the necessity to operate within a budget. In each case, a news organization attempts to insure a reasonable return—a usable story—for each economic investment that it makes. The network portfolio, its daily list of news assignments, does not consist of high-risk stocks. The network news portfolio is nearly all safe and reliable certificates of deposit from major city banks.

In more general terms, the homogeneity of television news is a function of the technological requirements and practices of television news. Persons and events in the news are selected and presented in those sites most amenable to visual formats.[4] The result is a convergence of stories and

---

[3]Epstein, E. J. (1973). *News from nowhere*. New York: Vintage Books.
[4]Altheide, D. L. (1985). *Media power*. Newbury Park, CA: Sage.

ideas in the news reports of the television networks. Nor is this convergence limited to television news. There is significant agreement among all the news media because they share a common set of professional news values. To a considerable degree, what you read in *The New York Times* is what you see on CBS. A comparison of nine news agendas in news magazines, newspapers, and television network broadcasts during the 1968 presidential election found a median correlation of + .79. A score of + 1.0 would indicate perfect agreement.[5] In short, there was remarkable agreement on the news of the day. Or put another way, each of these nine news organizations applied the professional values of journalism in a highly reliable manner. Furthermore, the similarities are strongest within each cluster of news media sharing a common technology. The news agenda of a television network is more like that of another network than of a newspaper. Newspapers are more like other newspapers than like television networks. But even with technological constraints, they are all very similar!

NEWS PEOPLE

Although the policies and personalities of formal organizations add the final layer of influence to the daily news, these news organizations, after all, are composed of individual men and women who enjoy considerable latitude in the way each news story is written and edited. The news is produced by news people, not by computers or other machines. The news is an intellectual product.

So having examined the outer layer, the sociology of organizational influences, we turn to the next layer, the social psychology of individual journalists. Two major sources of influence are to be considered at this layer of the onion: the socialization of journalists into their work and the individual differences that distinguish the behavior of one journalist from another.

News is the commodity of journalism and a sense of newsworthiness, the core professional instinct and talent of the journalist. Unlike a flair for mathematics or foreign languages, it is not an innate talent and instinct. A newsperson's sense of news must be learned and constantly honed, much like the putting skills of the professional golfer. The journalist who becomes a professional—defined here simply as someone who can produce acceptable copy for the daily news—must be socialized into the profession. Socialization means learning the values of the profession so well that they become an intellectual reflex when confronting the events of the day. The fact that competing newspapers, rival television networks, and contending news

---

[5]McCombs, M., & Shaw, D. (1972). The agenda-setting function of mass media. *Public Opinion Quarterly, 36*, 176–187.

magazines consistently produce highly similar news packages attests to the successful socialization into a single profession of myriad journalists working for distinct organizations.

When asked what factors are influential in determining their day-to-day judgments of newsworthiness, journalists most frequently cite their training, both in college courses and on the job. Both responses reflect lengthy and continuing acculturation to the norms of the profession. Other influences cited are staff colleagues, both supervisors and peers, and the performance of other news media. But, interestingly, these are ranked below the individual learning that results from college and experience in the news room.[6]

Although this experience in college and the news room tends to produce homogeneity, many individual differences remain. Professional views and values undoubtedly dominate the writing and editing of the news, but, after all, "reporters are humans who, like other humans, can never wholly escape the influence of their own opinions and emotions" (p. 651).[7] And these individual differences do influence the news stories crafted by reporters.[8]

For example, among newspaper reporters in Madison, Wisconsin, there were strong correlations between the personal opinions of those journalists and the number of favorable and unfavorable statements included in their stories on 13 contemporary public issues. Generally, these were not statements by the reporter, but rather statements obtained from news sources about these issues. Of course, none of these reporters produced news copy molded solely by his or her personal opinions. Numerous reference groups, including editors and professional peers, and numerous frames of reference, including the traditions of journalism and organizational policy, influenced the shape of each news story.[9]

When discussions of public affairs turn to journalism, the central theme usually is bias. And by bias people mean partisan political bias. This behavior could be located in either layer of the onion that we are peeling. That is, political bias can be organizational behavior, a deliberate policy of slanting the news to favor one group over another. Or, political bias can be individual behavior, one reporter's style of selecting or writing the news.

---

[6]Weaver, D., & Wilhoit, G. C. (1986). *The American journalist*. Bloomington: Indiana University Press.

For an overview of the research literature on the socialization of journalists, see Singletary, M. W. (1982). Commentary: Are journalists "professionals"?, *Newspaper Research Journal, 3*, 75–87.

[7]Charnley, M. V. *Reporting*. Quoted (p. 651) in Flegel, R. C., & Chaffee, S. H. (1971). Influences of editors, readers and personal opinions on reporters. *Journalism Quarterly, 48*, 645–651.

[8]For a detailed review of how journalists gather and organize information, see Stocking, S. H., & Gross, P. H. (1989). *How do journalists think?* Bloomington, IN: ERIC Clearinghouse on Reading and Communication Skills. Also see Reese and Shoemaker, op. cit., pp. 53–84.

[9]Flegel and Chaffee, op. cit.

At the organizational level, the overwhelming thrust of the accumulated evidence is that standards of fairness and balance are paramount in our daily reports of the news. Back in 1952 Democratic presidential candidate Adlai Stevenson remarked that America was a two-party country with a one-party press. The visible tip of the partisan press iceberg was the overwhelming editorial endorsement of Republican candidate Dwight Eisenhower by two thirds of the American dailies taking a stand in that election.

Of course, the explicit statement of an editorial opinion by a newspaper does not constitute bias. Newspapers certainly have the right to state openly their opinions and preferences for candidates and public policies on the editorial page. But many persons inferred that beneath the visible tip of editorial endorsements was a vast and dangerous mass of biased news reporting. Subsequent to Stevenson's observation, there was an outpouring of content analyses examining how daily newspapers—and, in subsequent decades, television—covered the Democratic and Republican presidential campaigns.

The overwhelming preponderance of the evidence from three decades now of accumulated research is that the major parties and their candidates are accorded fair and equal treatment. Little or no evidence of partisan political bias has been found in press coverage.[10] None of this contradicts the findings of the Wisconsin study, which found that individual attitudes do influence, to some degree, the selection of facts in individual stories. But the accumulated impact of these stories collectively—at least in political campaigns—is a balanced neutrality.

NEWS TRADITIONS

News reports overwhelmingly are fair and balanced because these criteria are the operational definitions of the overarching journalistic standard of objectivity in news reporting. But repeated findings of fairness and balance by no means establish the objectivity of the news in the fullest sense of that standard. There are biases in the daily news report. But they are not the commonly asserted partisan biases. Rather they are the structural biases that arise from the very nature of journalistic reporting and writing.[11] The narrative styles of journalism shape the configuration of facts reported in the news.

The behavior of individual journalists and the behavior of news organi-

---

[10]McCombs, M. (1972). Mass communication in political campaigns: Information, gratification and persuasion. In F. G. Kline & P. J. Tichenor (Eds.), *Current perspectives in mass communication research* (pp. 169–194). Beverly Hills: Sage.

[11]Hofstetter, C. R. (1976). *Bias in the news*. Columbus: Ohio State University Press.

zations do significantly influence the final shape of the daily news report. But it is important to remember that these individual and organizational influences are expressed through the genre of writing that we know as journalism. This genre, this style of writing, is the medium of exchange for the daily news. Only when we understand this inner core of the onion will we fully understand the role played by journalism in the creation of public opinion.

CHAPTER FOUR

Framing the News

Public opinion polls offer a representative picture of a community, state, or nation. Polls achieve this picture through the random interviewing of persons throughout the population. If journalists applied this same technique to news gathering, the results would be disastrously dull. This is because the public opinion poll's picture typically contains an extensive mixture of positive, negative and indifferent thoughts. Most news audiences are not very interested in reports about people who do not know or do not care one way or the other. They are not very interested in organizations or institutions who are not doing anything in particular—unless this in itself is evidence of serious neglect or irresponsibility. And, in fact, audiences generally are not all that interested in positive news when it consists of ordinary people and organizations engaged in their daily routine. In short, if the daily news net were cast to harvest a random sample of the day's events and situations, most of the yield would be routine and dull. This, in turn, would be disastrous for daily newspapers and television stations, who must maintain an interested, attentive audience in order to be economically viable as advertising media.

But, as Walter Lippmann pointed out more than a half century ago, journalists "do not try to keep an eye on all mankind . . . the news is not a mirror of social conditions, but the report of an aspect that has obtruded itself" (pp. 338–341).[1] The day's news is far from a random sample repre-

---

[1]Lippmann, W. (1922). *Public opinion*. New York: Macmillan.

senting the full history and behavior of our community, nation, or planet on that particular day. It is a report primarily of the odd and unusual and of people or institutions in conflict.[2] Furthermore, not all conflicts, not all unusual happenings have an equal chance of being reported in the daily news. In part, because their neat boundaries best fit the requirements of a daily news report that must be prepared on deadlines, discrete events rather than general situations and on-going trends are more commonly the focus of journalism. The limitations of this event-orientation among journalists have been commented on many times.[3] At this point, rather than to repeat these criticisms of reporting technique and practice, let us simply note that primary attention to deviant and discordant events is the predominant fact of life in contemporary journalism. This in no way says that it must be or that it should be. It just notes that it is! In terms of public opinion polling and the drawing of representative samples to represent a larger universe, the news represents a stratified sample of each day's history. From the myriad facts potentially available, only a single narrow stratum—deviant and discordant events—is heavily sampled.

Although discussions of this selection procedure usually concentrate on news values, more than professional values and attitudes are at work shaping what the reporter sees. To a considerable degree, what each reporter sees is framed by the genre in which he or she writes. Although news values and the tradition of objectivity emphasize the information content of the daily news, there is an equally strong tradition in journalism that prizes the dramatic and attention-maintaining quality—some would even say the entertainment value—of each news item.

A good news item, whether in the newspaper or on television, maximizes both information and drama. There are news items which score high on only one of these attributes—Charles Kuralt's poetic "On the Road" pieces and, in contrast, those interminably dreary reports on city council meetings and legislative sessions instantly come to mind. But these clearly are exceptions to the rule. Not every news item succeeds in framing its information in a dramatic cloak. But most try. The result, as we see here, is a particular—some would say, peculiar—diet of information about public affairs. The significant professional debate about this point for journalism is whether news balances information and entertainment qualities or whether it is a tension between information and entertainment.

---

[2]Shoemaker, P., Chang, T. K., & Brendlinger, N. (1987). Deviance as a predictor of newsworthiness: Coverage of international events in the U.S. media. In M. L. McLaughlin (Ed.), *Communication Yearbook 10* (pp. 348–365). Newbury Park, CA: Sage.

Shoemaker, P. (1987). The communication of deviance. In B. Dervin & M. J. Voight (Eds.), *Progress in communication sciences* (Vol. 8, pp. 151–175). Norwood, NJ: Ablex.

[3]McCombs, M., Shaw, D., & Grey, D. (1976). *Handbook of reporting methods* (pp. 3–19). Boston: Houghton Mifflin.

TELLING STORIES

In any event, increased attention has been paid recently to the form in which news appears, to the narrative style of reporting the day's news. "Part of the claim that news is a particular cultural genre or type, in the same sense as the novel, feature film or opera, rests on observations about the constancy, predictability and universality of the news form" (p. 144), noted communication theorist Denis McQuail.[4] He also underscored the relatively small differences between print news and TV news given the radical differences in the technologies and organizational structures of the two media.

Although there are some minor differences in style and in the operating procedures dictated by the nature of the medium employed to reach a mass audience, both newspapers and television assemble a daily news report composed of news stories. The common use of the term *story* is telling. Central to the genre of journalism is the story. In other words, a journalist functions both as a gatherer of facts and as a writer of stories. Journalism is a synergistic combination of observation and writing. And the genre of the writer exerts considerable influence on what he or she does as an observer.

Journalists are not neutral observers in the fullest sense of that term. What they observe—the particular facts they gather—is largely dictated by the story forms of journalism. Of course, people who were not looking for anything in particular would seldom find anything in particular. Guided by the traditional story forms of journalism, reporters look for the facts pertinent to these story forms.

Robert Darnton learned this during his first summer on the *Newark Star Ledger*.[5] On a day when there was little else to do, he wrote for practice a four-paragraph story about a young boy whose bicycle had been stolen. When Darnton showed his story, which was a straightforward recitation of the facts contained in a police report, to an experienced reporter on the police beat, the man replied that it was not really a *story* in that form. Quickly, the older journalist constructed a publishable story suggested by the meager facts in hand:

> Every week Billy put his twenty-five cent allowance in his piggy bank. He wanted to buy a bike. Finally, the big day came. He chose a shiny red Schwinn, and took it out for a spin in the park. Every day for a week he rode proudly around the same route. But yesterday three toughs jumped him in the middle of the park. . . . (p. 190)[6]

---

[4]McQuail, D. (1984). *Mass communication theory*. Beverly Hills: Sage.
[5]Darnton, R. (1975). Writing news and telling stories. *Daedalus, 104*, 175–194.
[6]Ibid., 190.

The situation dryly summarized in the police report had been reworked as a story in the real sense of that term. Darnton immediately was on the phone to gather the facts that were needed to tell this story. The experienced journalist had recognized an archetypal story in the facts of the police report. The job of the reporter was to acquire the facts necessary to flesh out the details of this archetype or paradigm. In short, the narrative form selected for this story determined the line of questioning with the news sources.

"Historians of American journalism—with the exception of Helen MacGill Hughes, a sociologist—seem to have overlooked the long-term cultural determinants of 'news' " (p. 189),[7] noted Darnton, who moved on from journalism to become a distinguished professor at Princeton. In fact, as a scholar, Darnton later came across an early nursery rhyme that bore a striking resemblance to his story of Billy's bike.

Darnton described the literary and cultural roots of several specific paradigms used by contemporary journalists to frame their stories. More generally, journalism professor Hunter P. McCartney has demonstrated that basic plot situations used over the centuries in literary works also are present in news stories.[8] One literary theory identifies 36 versions of five fundamental conflict situations, which are repeated, with unfailing distinctions, in all epochs and in all genres.[9] These genres include contemporary newspapers, television news programs, and news magazines. The situations most frequently found by McCartney in news stories across all three media were falling prey to misfortune ("200,000 at Rites for Polish Priest"), enigma ("Internal Split Blurs U.S. Policy on Nicaragua"), and supplication ("Hospital Panels Consider Key Ethics Issues"). Altogether, McCartney found 19 of the 36 classic conflict situations present in contemporary news stories.

AN INVENTORY OF THEMES

Taken to the extreme, reporters write totally stereotypical stories. In some cases, fact gathering is little more than asking the questions necessary to fill in the blanks. Lewis Lapham marveled at the ease and quickness with which a senior reporter turned out polished stories on the catastrophes of the day. Finally, the secret was revealed.

> In the drawer, with a bottle of bourbon and the manuscript of the epic poem he had been writing for twenty years, he kept a looseleaf notebook filled with stock versions of maybe fifty or sixty common newspaper texts. These were arranged in alphabetical order (fires, homicides, ship collisions, etc.) and then

---

[7]Ibid., 189.

[8]McCartney, H. P. (1987). Applying fiction conflict situations to analysis of news stories. *Journalism Quarterly, 64,* 163–170.

[9]Polti, G. (1931). *The thirty-six dramatic situations.* Boston: The Writer.

further divided into subcategories (fires—one-, two-, and three-alarm; warehouse; apartment building; etc.). The reporter had left blank spaces for the relevant names, deaths, numbers, and street addresses. As follows: "A—alarm fire swept through—at—St. yesterday afternoon, killing—people and causing— in property damage." (p. 37)[10]

But short of these fill-in-the-blanks stereotypes, which could easily lend themselves to computer-written stories, the inherited traditions of journalism provide each reporter with a lode of themes and story angles.

Some of these themes show a remarkable longevity. French historians have traced the reappearance across three centuries of a story about a case of mistaken identity in which parents murder their own son. First published in a Parisian news-sheet of 1618, this story made a number of 19th-century appearances in the provinces, and finally in a contemporary Algerian newspaper from which Albert Camus rewrote it in existentialist style for *L'Etranger* and *Malentendu*. Obviously, the names, dates, and places vary, but the generic story is unmistakably the same across all three centuries.[11]

Even Darnton, who reported this amazing historical succession, had the same experience on a minor scale. While working as a reporter, he came up with an idea for a story on policemen's horses, only to learn after its publication that his newspaper had carried the same story, more or less, at least twice during the previous decade.[12]

Sociologist Herbert Gans' extensive observations of major national news media identified seven themes that accounted for nearly all their foreign news. He noted that "foreign news deals with the same kinds of people and activities as domestic news, but since it does so in fewer and shorter stories, it also brings the priorities in domestic news into sharper focus" (p. 31).[13] Given the vast array of potential information from abroad, it is remarkable that only a handful of themes account for nearly all the coverage.

Timeliness, an emphasis on what is new, is a professional fetish in journalism. Nevertheless, no journalist takes an entirely fresh look at a new world of events each day. Journalists by virtue of their socialization into the profession—through college education and experience in the news room— work within an established narrative tradition. Each journalist inherits from his or her professional predecessors a sense of how the news is to be presented, a sense of how a news story is to be told.[14]

---

[10]Lapham, L. (1981, July). Gilding the news. *Harper's*, p. 35. Quoted in Bennett, W. L. (1988). *News: The politics of illusion* (2nd ed.). New York: Longman.

[11]Darnton, op. cit., p. 189.

[12]Ibid., 190.

[13]Gans, H. (1979). *Deciding what's news.* New York: Vintage Books.

[14]Stephens, M. (1988). *A history of news: From the drum to the satellite.* New York: Viking.

This received tradition is far more than a general orientation to the news of the day. As Darnton, Gans, and Lapham have pointed out, there is a substantial inventory of specific themes and generic stories to guide the framing of today's news. Some of these framing devices may be virtually timeless. Our very conception of news results from ancient ways of telling "stories." English chapbooks, broadside ballads, penny dreadfuls and French canards all purvey the same motifs as contemporary crime reporting in the newspaper. And although crime reporting and tabloid journalism may be more stylized than the writing that appears in *The New York Times*, nevertheless, there is considerable standardization and stereotyping there as well, Darnton observed from his own experiences as a journalist.

Undoubtedly, there is a strong strain of cultural determinism in contemporary news stories. Unfortunately, historians have yet to carefully examine the ebb and flow of particular themes and stories over time or to catch the introduction of new story elements. The kinds of stories told by journalists do change to some extent over time. But that is a task for another day.

FRAMING THE NEWS

Our purpose here simply is to recognize that journalists work within a genre with a lengthy history. The conventions of this genre and its specific inventory of stories influence the framing of the daily news. Our news of public affairs commonly is framed from the perspective of what makes a good story less than from the perspective of what makes a good citizen.[15] The news emphasizes those facts that advance the story. In part, this is why public officials often complain that the news media are not telling their story.

The President and the White House staff may have truly believed that the public needed to know every fact contained in the 132 handouts made available to the news media during a 4-week period in the summer of 1986. But to the journalists most of that material—68.9% to be specific—was not newsworthy.[16] There was no story there!

Of course, to return to the polling concept used at the beginning of this chapter, the information released from the White House press office was not a complete or fully representative picture of the presidency that summer. Although some of the information was released in news story form adhering

---

[15]*The Markle commission on the media and the electorate*. (1989). New York: John and Mary R. Markle Foundation.

[16]Turk, J. V. (1988). To know us is to love us: Do public relations messages really make a difference? *Southwestern Mass Communication Journal, 3*, 80–92.

Also see Turk, J. V. (1986). Information subsidies and media content. *Journalism Monographs, 100*.

to the conventions of journalism, the dominant perspective was not the narrative tradition of journalism, but rather the narrative tradition and rhetorical stance of politics. Each of these narrative traditions influences the selection of facts and frames those facts in such ways that they take on extra meaning from their context.

It becomes essential for the individual citizen who consumes these facts and stories to recognize these influences. When an array of facts are presented in a particular story frame, the whole can become more than the sum of its parts. Put in the extreme, the facts about public affairs commonly available to the general public are communicated in a journalistic genre which utilizes story forms not at all unlike those of fiction. E. L. Doctorow contended that there is neither fact nor fiction. There is only narrative![17]

---

[17]Quoted in Fishkin, S. (1985). *From fact to fiction. Journalism & imaginative writing in America*. Baltimore: Johns Hopkins University Press.

PART THREE

Reporting the News

Shaping the News Agenda

Drug abuse catapulted to the top of the news agenda during 1986. There were front-page stories in major newspapers, a news magazine cover story, and television specials. Public opinion polls reflected heightened public concern about drugs, and the politicians responded quickly. In just a matter of weeks, Congress wrote and passed anti-drug legislation backed by $1.7 billion in funding.

These trends in news coverage and public opinion across 1986 provide a concise portrait of the agenda-setting role of the news media for a very dramatic and emotional issue, drug abuse. In chapter 2 this influence of the mass media on public opinion was taken up in detail. Here our purpose is to understand how the news agenda itself is shaped. Those months of intensive news coverage on drug abuse provide a highly visible and striking portrait of agenda setting within the news media themselves. It is a revealing look at how the news agenda is shaped.

The immediate historical antecedent of all that news coverage on drugs appears to be a visit by Jesse Jackson in the Fall of 1985 to A. M. Rosenthal, then the executive editor of *The New York Times*. He later described Jackson's remarks about drugs and their devastating destruction on minorities as "moving and eloquent" (p. 1).[1] Subsequently, *The Times* assigned a reporter to cover drugs full time and on November 29 published

---

[1]Kerr, P. (1986, November 17). Anatomy of an issue: Drugs, the evidence, the reaction. *The New York Times*, p. 1.

its initial front-page story on crack, a new form of inexpensive cocaine just beginning to flood the country. The leadership role of *The New York Times* in American journalism—what we would term its *agenda-setting power*—is widely known.[2] With that initial foray on its front page, the topic of drugs was poised for a major position on the news agenda during the subsequent year.

The 1986 barrage of news coverage on cocaine and crack began with a *Newsweek* cover story in its March 17 issue. Two weeks later, *The New York Times* followed with a story on the blatant sale of crack in the Washington Heights neighborhood. The high point in this build-up of the drug issue on the news agenda was the simultaneous publication on Sunday, May 18, of lengthy articles in all three New York City newspapers, *The Times, Daily News,* and *Newsday*. No one has examined a broad random sample of the nation's daily newspapers to determine how rapidly coverage of illegal drugs diffused after this round of major press attention. But the *Washington Post* quickly followed suit, joined shortly by the *Los Angeles Times*. Cocaine coverage remained high in all the elite newspapers for the remainder of the year.[3]

Just as *The New York Times* coverage influenced the play of the cocaine story in other newspapers, in turn, all this newspaper coverage set the television news agenda. The grand finale in this 6-month barrage of drug coverage during 1986 occurred in September when both NBC and CBS broadcast specials on cocaine. CBS' 2-hour program, "48 Hours on Crack Street," utilized the talents of 50 people in the news department.

There is no question that cocaine occupied a major position on the news agenda during 1986. But why did this issue rise so dramatically during the middle months of 1986? Noting that the problem had been bad for decades and that a variety of government and academic studies showed no sudden increase in drug use that year, *The New York Times* raised the question, "Why now?," in a November 1986, front-page story.[4]

Part of the coverage did result from startling news events, the deaths only 8 days apart from cocaine intoxication of two young athletes. Len Bias, an All-American basketball player for the University of Maryland, died on June 19. Don Rogers, a football player for the Cleveland Browns, died on June 27. Much of the daily news in newspapers and on television is event-driven. Journalism has a strong orientation toward events rather than situations and trends. Many issues appear on the news agenda only when compelling events

---

[2]See the discussion of this point on p. 379 of Winter, J. P., & Eyal, C. H. (1981). Agenda-setting for the civil rights issue. *Public Opinion Quarterly, 45,* 376–383.

[3]Reese, S., & Danielian, L. (1989). Intermedia influence and the drug issue: Converging on cocaine. In P. Shoemaker (Ed.), *Communication campaigns about drugs: Government, media, and the public* (pp. 29–46). Hillsdale, NJ: Lawrence Erlbaum Associates.

[4]Kerr, op. cit.

force them there. Historically, the lack of civil rights for Blacks endured for decades with little or no media attention. But the eruption of lunch counter sit-in's, Freedom Rides, and countless demonstrations and marches provided the events that moved civil rights onto the front pages and into the evening network newscasts of the 1950s and 1960s. Even if Southern newspapers had considered ignoring or playing down these news events, the existence of a national television news agenda made both the public and the newspapers extremely aware of this issue.[5]

Although much of the daily news is event-driven, events themselves, even the dramatic occurrence of two deaths from cocaine within a short span of time, are insufficient to explain the sudden preoccupation of the elite press with illegal drugs. Plus, recall that there had been no change in the incidence of drug use and that *The New York Times*—and later, *Newsweek*—had "discovered" the drug issue months before the deaths of Len Bias and Don Rogers. There are two major lessons to be learned from these observations and from our 1986 case study, if you will, of the drug issue.

MIRROR THEORY

The mirror theory of journalism asserts that the function of the news media is to hold a mirror up to society and to reflect what is there. Journalists frequently describe their work in these terms, holding that they simply are reporting what is there for anyone to see. Although Walter Cronkite's famous closing, "And that's the way it is," seems to reflect this perspective, even the equally famous motto of *The New York Times*, "All the news that's fit to print," hedges on this point. The latter portion of this motto might even imply a moralistic judgment of news selection, although, in reality, standards of good taste and morality occupy a minor position among the myriad decisions made by editors and reporters in putting together the daily news report.

Mirror theory is a simplistic account of journalism that ignores the inherent necessity to select a few details of each day's history for presentation in the newspaper or on television.

Of necessity, there are many blank spots in the mirror that the news media hold up to reality. To begin with, there are inherent limitations on the capacity of all news channels—your daily newspaper, the 30-minute network evening news, even Cable News Network. Beyond the blank spots created by capacity that flaw mirror theory, there is an even more fundamental flaw imposed by the form of journalistic writing. Where journalists once tran-

[5]Brehm, J., & Cohen, A. (1962). *Explorations in cognitive dissonance* (pp. 269–298). New York: Wiley.

scribed public debates for their newspapers in the style of the Congressional Record, they now write stories. The transcribed facts and statements are rearranged and converted into an inverted pyramid or sometimes into a literal narrative, a story! Charles Dickens began his professional career as a writer transcribing the Parliamentary debates. But this novelist would be very much at home in today's journalism, writing political nonfiction stories from London or Washington that could rival the absorbing qualities of *Pickwick Papers* or *The Old Curiosity Shop*. It would be great journalism, but it would not be a mirror image of public affairs in the literal sense of that phrase. It is more appropriate to think of such reports—and the more mundane ones we see daily—as the result of a prism that refracts the light from a limited portion of reality. Metaphorically, the prism represents both the narrative forms of journalism and the practices, values and traditions—as well as the individuality and idiosyncracy—of the organizations and journalists who produce these reports.

In short, the first lesson to be noted in our case study of drug coverage during 1986 is that mirror theory is wholly inadequate to provide an explanation for the prominent position of cocaine on the news agenda. The corollary point is that although much news is event-driven—and that point itself is a telling refutation of mirror theory—events themselves, no matter how well they fit the traditional news values of journalism, are not always sufficient to move a topic on to the news agenda or to maintain a topic on the agenda. As was the case with cocaine, the news media may place an issue on its agenda without the kind of coincidental dramatic news events that might automatically push it onto every front page across the country. And, as was the case with the Vietnam war and urban riots of the 1960s, the news media may drop an item from its agenda prior to the issue's actual empirical peak. Coverage of Vietnam and urban riots, for example, actually peaked a year or two before they reached their climaxes.[6]

JOURNALISTIC LEADERSHIP

The second lesson to be learned from our case study of drug coverage in 1986 centers on the leadership role played by some news media in setting the news agenda. Discussions of journalistic leadership typically focus on the role of the news media in influencing the agenda of the general public or of policymakers. Here we are not talking about the role of journalists in facilitating the public affairs roles of others outside the news media. We are talking about leadership among the news media themselves.

---

[6]Funkhouser, G. R. (1973). The issues of the sixties: An exploratory study in the dynamics of public opinion. *Public Opinion Quarterly, 37*, 62–75.

Sociologist Warren Breed has described this dendritic influence of a few larger newspapers—and, occasionally, a news magazine or television network—on the remainder of the news media.[7] Like the evolution of a family tree, this arterial flow from a leader to a coterie of followers has a number of different patterns. Sometimes the influence is direct and the behavior of the followers, pure imitation. For example, noting the close professional competition between *The New York Times* and *The Herald Tribune* during the 1960s, Richard Kluger described the close watch kept by *The Times* on the news play of the circulation-trailing *Herald Tribune*. It was not unusual for *The Times'* managing editor to order changes in the front-page makeup after seeing the early edition of *The Herald Tribune*.[8]

Others have noted how wire service budgets of the day's major stories influence the layout of newspapers across the nation. But wire service influence is far more pervasive than just the play of major stories or the makeup of the front page. A study of how Iowa dailies used the Associated Press (AP) found that local news agendas were strongly influenced by the wire service report. Of course, each local newspaper used only a small number of the stories available from the wire. But their coverage reflected essentially the same proportions for each category of news as did the wire report.[9] In essence, the AP set the agenda of the local newspapers.

Both of these patterns of influence, imitating layout and general coverage, are direct and immediate. Our case study of the 1986 drug coverage reflects a longer term influence on the salience of topics in the news. Sometimes this longer term influence is just a matter of an editor getting ideas for a subsequent story. Obviously, the assignment editors for the networks read *The New York Times* and other major newspapers each day. And so do the editors of *Time* and *Newsweek*.

But sociologist Breed's concept extends far beyond the elite news media in New York and Washington. The arterial flow that he described is more complex, resembling a tangled family tree of news diffusion. Story ideas frequently originate in one of the elite news media and initially diffuse to other elites. Then the coverage reaches down to the major regional dailies, newspapers like the *Dallas Morning News* and *Minneapolis Tribune*; then on to the middle-size and smaller dailies. Although these diffusion patterns have been described anecdotally many times, the exact dynamics for the diffusion of new topics on the public affairs agenda of the news media are not fully known.

---

[7]Breed, W. (1980). *The newspaperman, news and society*. New York: Arno Press.

[8]Kluger, R. (1986). *The paper. The life and death of the New York Herald Tribune*. New York: Alfred A. Knopf.

[9]Gold, D., & Simmons, J. L. (1965). News selection patterns among Iowa dailies. *Public Opinion Quarterly, 29*, 425–430. Also see Whitney, C., & Becker, L. (1982). Keeping the gates for gatekeepers: The effects of wire news. *Journalism Quarterly, 59*, 60–65.

However, the fact that it happens is hardly surprising. Nor is there anything sinister or conspiratorial in this pattern of diffusion. Many of the decisions that we make in our daily behavior, either as individuals or as institutions, are made under ambiguous circumstances. Observers of human behavior from Plato to the authors of the latest textbook on social psychology have noted our need for social support of our actions. If you aren't convinced on this point, observe the behavior of teen-age high school students. Their desire for social support is often rampant! It is hardly surprising, then, that the editors of newspapers and television news programs also seek social support for their decisions about what are the important news stories of the day.

In selecting that very small number of events and topics to observe and report, editors are guided to a considerable degree by news values. They tend to seek out stories high on three key dimensions:[10]

- significance, impact, and magnitude;
- obtrusiveness, conflict, or oddity;
- high status persons.

But the application of news values to the myriad events and situations in the world is far from unambiguous. We are far from the point where a computer could be programmed to make daily news assignments or to select stories for the daily news report. The remark is still made too often that journalists may not be able to define news, but they know it when they see it. Actually, it is an inaccurate saying. Most journalists frequently look over their shoulders to make sure they have not strayed too far from other journalists' application of news values to the day's events. In the extreme, this has been called "pack journalism."[11]

Seeking social support and verification for professional judgments about the news of the day is not unusual behavior, especially when a decision about how to lead a story has to be made in a highly ambiguous situation. That was the case during the 1972 Iowa caucuses in which George McGovern suddenly emerged as a major Democratic candidate because the lead of *The New York Times'* R. W. Apple proclaimed him so.[12]

Individuals working in a social setting, as were those journalists in Iowa, often follow the lead of their colleagues. In a famous experiment by social psychologist Solomon Asch,[13] subjects drastically altered their judgments of

---

[10]Baddii, N., & Ward, W. J. (1980). The nature of news in four dimensions. *Journalism Quarterly, 57,* 243–248.

[11]Crouse, T. (1972). *The boys on the bus.* New York: Ballentine.

[12]Ibid., 84–85.

[13]Asch, S. (1962). Effects of group pressure upon the modification and distortion of judgments. In D. Cartwright & A. Zander (Eds.), *Group dynamics* (pp. 189–200). Evanston, IL: Row, Peterson.

the comparative lengths of two lines—a thoroughly objective task—in the face of overwhelming contrary judgments by their peers in the experiment. Of course, the peers, unknown to the subject, were parties to a conspiracy. But the effects of social support—or, in that case, a lack of social support for the experimental subject's judgment—were clearly demonstrated.

Nor is it unusual for individuals working in a social setting to accede to the judgments of higher status individuals. That was the case in Iowa. *The Times'* Apple set the agenda for the next-day news coverage on the outcome of the Iowa primary with its implications for the Presidential election. As Crouse described the scene, the other reporters present literally grouped themselves around Apple in rows of descending status: "The AP guy was looking over one shoulder, the UPI guy over the other and CBS, NBC, ABC and the Baltimore Sun were all crowding in behind" (p. 84).[14]

SETTING THE AGENDA

It is not entirely clear why *The New York Times* has achieved the status and eminence among journalists that it now enjoys. Historically, it has not always been the pre-eminent leader of American journalism. However, its status is such now that other reporters often leak original ideas and information to *Times* reporters so that its appearance there validates the story as major news.

Although the origins of *The Times'* status are obscure, it is not surprising that the major agenda setters in American journalism are located primarily in New York and Washington. Despite the steady movement of the population center of the United States to the west and south and despite the dispersion of wealth, as measured by the geographic locations of the largest banks and headquarters of the major corporations, New York and Washington remain the power centers of this country. Much of the cultural, political, and economic leadership emanates from those cities, and the news media located there have access to many of the most powerful and knowledgeable news sources. As we learn more about the diffusion of major news topics within the news media, it will be interesting to see the extent to which other cities share this agenda-setting leadership.

---

[14]Crouse, op. cit., p. 84.

CHAPTER SIX

Exposure to News

Central in the tradition of democratic societies is the myth of the omniscient citizen. Although the fallacies of this assumption about civic competence and interest in public affairs already have been sketched, it is important to note here that neither democratic theory nor democratic practice rests solely upon—to put it in the extreme—a naive assumption about human behavior. In many ways, this assumption is best regarded as a social goal rather than as an assertion about human behavior and potential. Historically, this broad social goal has been operationalized in such specific government and community programs as universal education and literacy, which took root in the early days of our republic, and, more recently, literacy and competency tests for graduating high school seniors to ensure that our elementary and secondary schools are achieving the desired educational goals.

But, as we might say about a good law, democratic theory also has some teeth in it. Rather than being limited to the statement of an assertion or expression of a goal, there also are social norms embedded in our civic culture that provide impetus for matching theory with actual practice. Foremost among these norms is that cliché of democracy: A good citizen is an informed citizen. This normative statement sets a standard for each of us by restating the assumption of an informed citizen as an imperative. To be a *good* citizen, it says, you *must* be informed. Although no one sports a bumper sticker or tee shirt with this slogan, it is a familiar part of our political culture. It is so accepted that it remains implicit much of the time, articulated primarily by elementary school teachers and high school civics instructors in front of their classes. The authors' only recent explicit encounter with this social norm as an unadorned statement was at a museum replica of a turn-of-the-century school room.

But the impact of this norm is illustrated daily by the millions of Americans who read newspapers and watch television news programs. If one accepts this cultural norm that a good citizen is an informed citizen, then, by inference, one has a civic duty to keep up with the news. Although, in theory, every citizen should feel obliged to keep up with the news, in practice many do not! There are tremendous individual differences in the acceptance of this civic duty to keep up with the news. A majority have reasonably strong beliefs about this civic duty. But, put the other way, a significant minority of adults feel little or no obligation to keep up with the news.

The perceived nature of this civic obligation is well illustrated by some of the statements used in scientific studies to measure the strength of this belief. Nearly everyone is willing to endorse the broad concept of a civic duty: "We all have a duty to keep ourselves informed about news and current events." But when this norm is stated in a more tolerant way, fewer agree: "It is important to be informed about news and current events." And when surveys measuring this belief offer statements that give people an "out," large numbers take it: "So many other people follow the news and keep informed about it that it doesn't matter much whether I do or not"; and "A good deal of news about current events isn't important enough to keep informed about."

Not only have scholarly inquiries succeeded in measuring individual and community differences in this civic belief, research has documented that this belief is correlated with reading daily newspapers and viewing television news!

Among persons with a strong belief to keep up with the news, 75% are regular readers of a daily newspaper. They read the paper just about everyday. But as belief in this civic norm decreases, so does the frequency of newspaper reading. Among persons with weak beliefs, only about 50% regularly read a daily newspaper. Although this lower percentage of regular readers demonstrates the influence of this democratic norm on everyday behavior, it also documents the habitual character of newspaper reading among Americans. Even about 50% of those individuals who feel little civic compulsion to keep up with the news still read a newspaper just about everyday.

Both of these observations, the influence of civic norms and the habitual character of newspaper reading, also are supported by data on nonreaders—those persons who do not read a daily newspaper even one or two times a week. Such persons are all but nonexistent among strong believers in the duty to keep informed. But among persons with little belief in this duty, about one in seven is a nonreader.

Civic beliefs also are linked to television viewing. Regular viewing of network television news increases with the strength of these civic beliefs. Only 25% of those with weak civic beliefs view network evening news on television everyday. Among those with strong civic beliefs, about 50% view everyday. This empirical finding also helps define the nature of this civic norm and how it is translated into everyday behavior. Although the strength of these civic beliefs is strongly correlated with the frequency of both daily newspaper reading and viewing national television news, there is no correlation between these beliefs and the use of local television news or weekly newspapers.

The tilt toward national and international news in these findings is striking. It can be argued that the substantive meaning of these civic beliefs in terms of newspaper reading is ambiguous because newspapers contain large measures of both local and national–international news, plus entertainment features and advertising. But the correlations with other news media underscore the importance of national–international news in this relationship, suggesting the cosmopolitan character of this civic-inspired media exposure in contemporary life. That is a major shift of almost 180 degrees from the locally involved citizen of classic democratic theory.

In short, the contemporary evidence[1] is impressive that normative beliefs about civic duty are translated into daily practice. Use of mass communication to keep up with current affairs is the major mode of civic and political participation in our society today.

HISTORICAL TRENDS

What is lacking from the scholarly examination of civic duty is any evidence on the long-term trends in the strength of these beliefs. Social commentators have speculated on—and sometimes documented—declines and dramatic shifts in many other social norms during the last half of the 20th century. Has the civic obligation to keep up with the news suffered a similar fate? Although direct evidence is lacking on this question, there is abundant long-term empirical evidence on the expression of this norm in everyday behavior.

Historically, reading a daily newspaper has been the most common outcropping of these civic beliefs. It has continued to be a major indicator even with the major role played by network television news over the past three or four decades. But the continuing decline in regular newspaper reading and, more recently, in viewing television news is discouraging to

---

[1]McCombs, M., & Poindexter, P. (1983). The duty to keep informed: News exposure and civic obligation. *Journal of Communication, 33*, 86–88.

anyone who strongly believes that we all have a duty to be informed citizens and to keep up with the news.

By the middle of the 19th century there was true mass communication of news in the United States. The advent of mass circulation newspapers, launched by Benjamin Day's *New York Sun* and other members of the penny press in the 1830s, resulted in a total daily newspaper circulation exceeding 750,000 by 1850. To put those numbers in perspective, the United States at that time had only about 3.5 million households. In other words, daily newspaper penetration was about one household in five. The level of penetration continued to increase through the remainder of the 19th century. The Civil War generated both major journalistic innovations and high interest in timely news. Toward the end of the century, bold entrepreneurs like William Randolph Hearst and Joseph Pulitzer stimulated interest in the news—and, not incidentally, circulation—through sensational coverage and assertive promotion. Newspaper circulation and penetration continued to advance, and newspaper circulation soon exceeded the number of households. By 1910 there were 1.36 copies of a daily newspaper being sold for every household in the United States.

But somewhere in the years encompassing World War I the newspaper peaked as a mass medium in the United States. Although daily circulation increased another 3.5 million between 1910 and 1920, the ratio of circulation to households declined slightly. In 1910 the ratio had been 1.36. By 1920 it was 1.34, the beginning of a slow, but steady, decline interrupted only by the thirst for information during the days of World War II. But it was only a temporary halt and reversal of the decline.

In 1969 the ratio was 1.0 again. Daily newspaper circulation and the number of households once more had reached parity, their meeting point on the way up at the beginning of this century. In 1970 the ratio was .99, and the gap between circulation and population growth continued to widen.

The 1970s were a particularly troublesome time for America's newspaper publishers. Despite the fact that the aggregate penetration level of daily newspapers in the United States had been on the decline for more than a half century, until the 1970s publishers could take solace in the fact that aggregate circulation, with few exceptions, continued to increase year after year. But in 1975 even that boon disappeared. In 1973 total daily newspaper circulation stood at an all-time high: 63,147,000 copies. In 1974 circulation was down by more than 1 million copies. In 1975 circulation was down again by more than another million copies.

To put it another way, from an all-time high in 1973, daily newspaper circulation declined nearly 2.5 million copies in 2 years. In 1975 circulation was only 300,000 copies higher than it had been 10 years earlier. This precipitous drop bottomed out in 1975, and circulation began a slow climb back up. But in the meantime, the penetration of daily newspapers in the marketplace, the ratio of circulation to households, continued to drop. By 1985 penetration stood at .72 and by 1990 at .67.

Now in part the sharp decline of newspaper penetration in recent decades is an artifact of the way in which penetration is measured. Although the household is a natural and functional context for examining newspaper circulation, use of the number of households as the denominator in the penetration measure makes the resulting ratio subject to the effects of changes in the size of households in the United States over time.

Over the past 25 years the average American household has shrunk dramatically. In 1960 the average household consisted of 3.33 persons. By 1985 it was 2.69 persons. Even if newspaper circulation and the population had remained constant—or if circulation and population had grown by identical numbers—the rapidly expanding number of households due to increasingly smaller households would have resulted in lower and lower penetration statistics.

This is not to say that there has been no real decline in the diffusion of newspapers. It simply says that the decline is exaggerated by the rapid expansion in the number of households. When circulation is measured relative to the total population, we still witness a decline. It just is not quite as steep! Newspaper circulation per 1,000 population was 328 in 1960. By 1985 it was 269, a decline of 15%, compared to a decline of 36% in the penetration ratio during those 25 years. Either way, it was a downward trend.

Of course, every indicator has its limitations. Measuring the diffusion of newspapers among the general public by the ratio of circulation to the number of households, or even to the population, has several flaws. In order to understand fully this downward trend in the use of newspapers to keep up with the news, an alternative, more behavioral, measure of newspaper use also should be considered.

In recent decades the newspaper industry has cited a "read yesterday" statistic to indicate the diffusion of newspapers in terms of actual behavior. This label is a shorthand version of the question used by Market Research Bureau in annual national surveys: "Did you read a daily newspaper yesterday?"

Two decades ago, 75% of American adults had read a daily newspaper on the previous day. By 1990, 62.4% of the population reported reading a daily newspaper on the previous day.

Similar declines are occurring among the television news audience. There was a general decline during the 1980s for the broadcast networks as a whole, largely attributable to cable television. The decline has been even worse for the networks' evening news programs.

Within these broad downward trends for newspaper readership and TV news viewing, there are particularly significant declines among young adults ages 18–35. In both instances, the decline among young adults in the news audience is significantly greater than the overall downward trend.

Consistently across past decades, a smaller percentage of young adults had read a newspaper the previous day compared to the total population. In 1967, 76% of all Americans had read a daily newspaper the previous day. But only 71% of young adults, ages 18–24, and 73% of those ages 25–34 had read a newspaper the previous day. By 1986 the national figure had declined to 63%, as previously noted. But among those ages 18–24 the figure was now little more than half (53%), and among those ages 25–34, only 58%. The decline in "yesterday readership" among young adults exceeded the overall national decline.

But the "read yesterday" statistic merges everyday readers and occasional readers who happened to have read the day before. When we separate these groups, we find that up to 1975 young adults ages 18–30 had lower percentages of everyday readers than the overall national average; and the older age groups, a higher percentage of everyday readers. But from 1977 on, the age groups with lower than average percentages of everyday readers are both the 18–30 group and the 31–43 group. In other words, young adults who read newspapers less frequently during their early years—due in large measure to the transient nature of the early adult years—formerly showed an upswing in newspaper reading by age 30. That upswing is now being delayed into their 30s and early 40s.

Although there has been some speculation that the decline in both newspaper readership and TV news viewing is the product of one or two aberrant generations—the baby boomers, the me generation, Vietnam-era teen-agers, or whatever—detailed analysis of these trends suggests that the changes are permanent. This is not to assert that decreased exposure to news will result in a wholly uninformed citizenry. For example, the proportion of infrequent readers who look at a newspaper less than once a week has not changed very much in recent times. What has changed is the number of occasional readers. Americans are not abandoning newspapers, but more and more of them are drawn to them only occasionally during the week rather than everyday.

SEARCH FOR CULPRITS

With the decline in newspaper circulation and readership, editors and publishers cast about for explanations—and for culprits. Due to its prominence in American homes and behavior, not to mention its prominence on the pages of American newspapers, television was quickly indicted. After all, television had rapidly saturated American households in the 1950s and commandeered several hours a day of the typical adult's leisure time. Also recall that evening newspapers suffered especially during the late 1970s and 1980s. As late as 1975, PM circulation was 10 million higher than AM circulation. But by 1980, the lead had been reduced 66%, and in 1982, for the first time in the history of daily journalism, morning circulation surpassed evening circulation.

Close empirical scrutiny of the newspaper and television audiences, however, has rebutted the arguments that television is the culprit behind declining newspaper readership and circulation. First, we already have noted parallel declines over the last decade among both newspaper and TV news audiences. And the decline in newspaper circulation began decades before television ever appeared. More importantly, there is a substantial overlap in the audiences for newspapers and television news. Most people do not rely on a single source of information, but routinely consume a variety of news media. Prior to television the major example of this behavior was the two-newspaper reader, the "news junkie" who read both a morning and evening newspaper and probably several serious magazines each month. There are not very many two-newspaper readers these days, but there is considerable overlap in the audiences for the local daily newspaper and television news.

Across all news media, 91% of American adults interviewed in a national survey were exposed to some news "yesterday."[2] The largest group (25%) were exposed to all three news media: newspapers, television, and radio. The second most prevalent pattern (23%) was combined exposure to newspapers and television. Ignoring radio and concentrating only on newspapers and TV, a near majority of the population (48%) had used both newspapers and TV on the previous day. An additional 19% each used only newspapers or only television. Use of multiple media to keep up with the news clearly is the modal pattern of behavior for Americans.

If we look at the two "minority" groups, those groups of 19% each who use only newspapers or only television, there are some demographic differences. Persons with less than a high school education or an annual income less than $10,000 are twice as likely to use TV only than newspapers only. Conversely, college graduates and persons earning $35,000 + are twice as likely to use newspapers only. But in all four of these demographic categories, as well as in all the other education and income categories, the modal pattern, by far, is use of both news media. In the other education and income groups, the minorities using only newspapers or only television are about equal in size.

Further evidence that television is not the culprit behind the decline in newspaper readership is found in communication researcher Leo Bogart's

---

[2]*Newspapers in American news habits: A comparative assessment.* (1985). New York: Newspaper Advertising Bureau.

comparisons of TV news audience ratings with the newspaper circulation trends in the same communities. Overall, higher TV news ratings were associated with circulation gains, not losses. In 22 competitive markets, those with newspaper circulation gains actually had higher TV ratings than did communities experiencing a lack of circulation increases or the disappearance of a local daily.[3]

The 13-week 1978 New York newspaper strike yields even stronger evidence. Contrary to any belief that television has damaged newspaper readership—and particularly contrary to the common-sense hypothesis that the absence of newspapers would enhance the audience for TV news—a Newspaper Advertising Bureau study found that the ratings for network television news actually declined during the lengthy strike. Although the ratings did hold steady for local news, they actually improved once the New York City newspapers resumed publication.[4]

In short, there is no direct evidence to justify the indictment of television as the culprit behind the decline in newspaper reading. To the contrary, the evidence suggests that reading a newspaper and viewing television news are positively correlated.

Finally, the most pervasive myth of all about television news and newspapers must be dispelled. Contrary to widespread belief and the frequent citation of "supportive" polling data, the majority of Americans do not receive most of their news from TV. This myth about the pervasiveness of TV news can be traced to the frequently cited polls for the Television Information Office, which ask: "I'd like to ask you where you usually get most of your news about what's going on in the world today. . . ." In 1959, when this question was first asked of a national sample, 51% cited television. There has been a steady increase in the proportion mentioning TV ever since, and newspapers have been left trailing far behind.

But, commented *TV Guide* writer Joanmarie Kalter:

> Trouble is, that innocent poll question is downright impossible to answer. Just consider: It asks you to sort through the issues in your mind, pinpoint what and where you learned about each, tag it, and come up with a final score. Not too many of us can do it, especially since we get our news from a variety of sources. Even pollster Burns concedes, "Memories do get fuzzy."
>
> Scholars have found, however, that when they ask a less general, more specific question—Did you read a newspaper yesterday? Did you watch a TV news show yesterday?—the results are quite different. Dr. John Robinson, professor of sociology at the University of Maryland, found that on a typical

---

[3]Bogart, L. (1989). *Press and public* (2nd ed.). Hillsdale, NJ: Lawrence Erlbaum Associates. Also see Moore, B. A., Howard, H. H., & Johnson, G. C. (1988). TV news viewing and the decline of the afternoon newspaper. *Newspaper Research Journal, 10*, 15–24.

[4]*Ibid.*, 249–251.

day 67 per cent read a newspaper, while 52 per cent see a local or national TV newscast. (p. 3)[5]

Another explanation for declining news audiences focused on younger adults. The evidence generally cited here is national test scores suggesting a lesser ability to read among younger adults. Most critics also point out that these are the generations who grew up with television entertainment. The evidence is unequivocally clear that they do not read newspapers—or view television news—with anywhere near the frequency that their parents did. In 1990 only one young adult in three had "read a newspaper yesterday," about half the proportion in their parents' generation. The TV news picture is similar, about two out of five young adults, compared to two out of three adults age 50 and older, had "watched TV news yesterday" during 1990.

But young adults do consume mass communication. National data reported by Market Research Bureau shows magazine readership among young adults age 18–24 that is double the level for newspapers. Among persons ages 25–34, the magazine readership scores are more than 75% higher than the newspaper readership scores. Only in the 35–44 age group is there parity between magazine and newspaper readership. In the older age groups, newspapers prevail. Bogart also noted that young adults under age 35 account for double their share of paperback book purchases and over 40% more than their share of hard cover books. They may not be reading newspapers, but they are reading!

Unfortunately, a recent study of social trends across the past half century reports that the young audience has buoyed the popularity of the new, lighter media forms, such as *People* magazine and TV's "A Current Affair." Aptly titled *The Age of Indifference*,[6] this report states that young Americans know less, care less, and use news media less than any generation in the past five decades. Surveys conducted in the 1940s, 1950s, and 1960s indicate that all generations were equally interested in major stories like the McCarthy hearings and the Vietnam War. But for recent news events, only 12% of those ages 18–29 followed news about the federal bail out of the savings and loans very closely, compared to 36% of those age 50 and older. For the opening of the Berlin Wall, the comparative percentages are 42% versus 58%. But for the Super Bowl, as one might expect, the pattern reverses: 27% of young adults versus 18% of older Americans.

All the discussions so far in this chapter have centered on the major news media, local daily newspapers, and network television news. There are the minor, albeit high quality, specialized news media, such as public broad-

---

[5]Kalter, J. (1987, May 30). Exposing media myths. *TV Guide 35*(22), 3.

[6]*The age of indifference*. (1990). Los Angeles: Times Mirror Center for the People and the Press.

casting and the news and opinion magazines. But these remain elite news media. And, of course, there also is the opportunity to participate vicariously in such public affairs events as the campaign debates, national political conventions, major Congressional hearings, and the annual State of the Union address. But in terms of the national audience, both in size and demographics, these are experiences far beyond the ken of most American voters.

LINKING MEDIA USE AND KNOWLEDGE

Although the amount of public affairs knowledge possessed by individual citizens sometimes is less than fully impressive, nevertheless there is widespread belief in a civic duty to keep informed. And, to a considerable degree, these beliefs are translated into exposure to the mass media. There is a large daily audience for television news and newspapers, even though the audience for newspapers has been steadily shrinking since World War I. Beyond these general patterns that have been sketched in this chapter, what else can we say about the precise roles of newspapers and television in public affairs?

Television news is used more for general surveillance, whereas newspapers are used for more in-depth information. These functions of the news media are dramatically illustrated by the diffusion of major news events. Nearly everyone learned about the assassination of President John F. Kennedy from television or immediately turned to television after hearing the news from a friend. Only later did people turn to newspapers and news magazines for greater understanding of this tragedy. Much of the same pattern occurred more recently for the ill-fated launch of the spaceship Challenger.

Even for less salient events in the news, such as Cincinnati's cinch of the 1990 World Series in the fourth game, television takes the lead in spreading the initial word. But for events of this magnitude, many people also quickly turn to newspapers for more details and discussion.

Numerous scholarly studies have found that regular use of daily newspapers is associated with increased knowledge of public affairs. Most of these empirical investigations also examined television use and concluded that exposure to newspapers is more strongly correlated with increased public affairs knowledge than is exposure to television news.[7] One study even found that the association between space devoted to a topic in the newspaper and recall of information about that topic is stronger than the association between amount of time devoted to a topic on television and recall of in-

---

[7]Weaver, D., & Buddenbaum, J. (1979). Newspapers and television: A review of research on uses and effects. *ANPA News Research Report* (No. 19).

formation.[8] But *attention* to television news and newspapers has been found to predict public affairs knowledge about equally.[9] The news media are our windows on the world.

---

[8]Booth, A. (1970–1971). The recall of news items. *Public Opinion Quarterly, 34*, 604–610.

[9]Chaffee, S. H., & Schleuder, J. (1986). Measurement and effects of attention to media news. *Human Communication Research, 13*, 76–107.

PART FOUR

Imagining the News

Knowledge of
Public Affairs

Three important elements are involved in opinion formation: knowledge of the world, the media as the principal conduit and interpreter of that world, and the public. The public is not a passive audience. The public mind is not a *tabula rasa* waiting to be written on by the media.[1] Media messages are transformed by people's personal experiences, their motivations and interest in seeking additional information. What people know about public affairs also is constrained by structural factors, such as the accessibility of the media and their diversity of content.

In the cradle of democracy, the Greek polis, knowledge of public affairs was assumed as a prerequisite to informed participation. At that time, this was easier said—and done—than today. Communities were small and the citizenry quite homogenous—slaves and women were excluded, of course. We still like to think that informed participation is the lifeblood of democratic politics, but our assumptions are tempered by the size and complexity of communities today and by our understanding of constraints on the public's ability to know.

The terms *knowledge* and *information* are used often in this chapter, and it might be helpful if we described what both terms mean. Information is the bits or pieces on which knowledge is based, or the building blocks

---

[1]Rosengren, K. E., Werner, L. A., & Palmgreen, P. (Eds.). (1985). *Media gratifications research*. Beverly Hills, CA: Sage.

of knowledge. Fritz Machlup called information "an increment to knowledge" (p. 19).[2]

This relationship is premised in William James' distinction between knowledge *of* and knowledge *about*. A simplified version of this distinction is that there is clearly much less information involved when one knows *of* something than when one is knowledgeable *about* the same thing.

In addition to implying quantity of information, knowledge has other dimensions. Those include the use of categories into which information bits are organized as well as salience, or the relative degree of importance or significance attached to topics, categories, actors, and so forth. Finally, knowledge implies awareness of possible choices or alternatives, or, when framed in terms of a problem, awareness of solutions.

If we take U.S. policy in the 1980s toward Nicaragua as an example, many individuals might have been aware of the "problem" that Nicaragua had posed for the United States. Some might have been familiar to some degree with the major actors, including the Contras, the Sandinistas, Daniel Ortega, Violeta Chamorro, and so forth. A smaller number of individuals would have had a hazy idea about the conflict between the Sandinistas and the Contras and whose side the United States had supported, and that some form of military aid had been supplied for some time.

Still fewer would have known about the significance of Nicaragua to overall U.S. foreign policy in Central America, of the foreign policy options that were available to the United States then, including such nonmilitary options as the Contadora Process, the historical background to the Sandinista–Contra conflict, and so forth. Overall, with this example, we are talking about significant differences in the quantity and quality of information, meaningful categorization of the information, salience of the various elements, and potential solutions.

LEARNING FROM THE NEWS

Do the news media have an impact on what we know? Most definitely! And the media can have some very important input into all four aspects of knowledge. News, as Robert Park maintained, *is* a form of knowledge.[3] But, unlike Park, we do not think that the news merely orients people. It is more than knowledge *of*. The mass media today are much more complex, diverse, and specialized than they were four decades ago and can certainly

---

[2]Machlup, F. (1980). *Knowledge: Its creation, distribution, and economic significance. Vol 1: Knowledge and knowledge production.* Princeton, NJ: Princeton University Press.

[3]Park, R. (1940). News as a form of knowledge. *American Journal of Sociology, 45,* 669–686.

provide information about many things, enough so that knowledge *about* events or issues can be achieved.

Interviewing a group of voters over several months led political scientist Doris Graber to conclude:

> Over time, the media do turn out to be effective providers of most of the information people need, given their desire to learn. Our panelists had learned specific details about the most prominent current news stories and had at least hazy recollections of the rest . . . (p. 78)[4]

Outside the political realm, one issue currently causing much concern is the AIDS (Acquired Immune Deficiency Syndrome) epidemic. The news media constitute the primary source of information about AIDS for most individuals, particularly those not among the high-risk groups. Those at risk will use a greater variety of sources and will engage in more active information seeking. But the news media have been primarily responsible for educating the public about various aspects of the disease, including how it is transmitted, who is most susceptible, and how to avoid it.

Having said this, we hasten to add an important caveat: Information availability does not automatically guarantee knowledge. As we know from chapter 6, no audience is guaranteed for the messages of the mass media. When social scientists have explored the question, "How much does the public know about public affairs?", the answers have not been very encouraging, particularly for those who adhere to the notion that the informed citizenry required for participatory democracy must include as many citizens as possible.[5]

A classic illustration of this dismal knowledge level is a 1950 study that found that a majority of individuals in a midwestern community still knew very little about the United Nations despite a 6-month information campaign.[6] In the years since that study, two important things have been learned about the diffusion of knowledge among members of the public. First, some people are much better informed than others. Second, some individuals *gain* information at a faster rate than others. The "public" actually consists of distinct groups with different knowledge levels and different degrees of political participation.[7]

[4]Graber, D. (1984). *Processing the news: How people tame the information tide*. New York: Longman.

[5]Buchanan, B. (in press). *Electing a president*. Austin: University of Texas Press.

[6]Star, S., & Hughes, H. M. (1950). Report on an educational campaign: The Cincinnati plan for the United Nations. *American Journal of Sociology, 55*, 389–400.

[7]Tichenor, P. J., Donohue, G., & Olien, C. (1970). Mass media and differential growth in knowledge. *Public Opinion Quarterly, 34*, 158–170.

Also see The knowledge gap hypothesis. In W. J. Severin & J. W. Tankard, Jr. (Eds.), *Communication theories* (2nd ed., pp. 285–299). New York: Longman.

In examining foreign policy publics, Gabriel Almond noted an *attentive* and *nonattentive* public.[8] Members of the attentive public for an issue possessed: (a) a high level of interest in the issue; (b) a functional level of knowledge about the issue; and (c) a pattern of regular information acquisition about the issue. This attentive group often has been called the political elite.

In using the Almond model to identify publics for science and technology issues, Jon Miller found that the attentive public was about one fifth of the adult population.[9] These were the individuals who expressed a high level of interest in science, who demonstrated a moderately high level of knowledge, were likely to follow science policy debates or issues and, even for a few, to participate in or to provide input for public policy formulation. These latter few represent the mobilized segment within the attentive public. Most persons, even among the attentive public, are a nonmobilized constituency for any particular issue.

A similar pattern was found during the 1976 election campaign. An attentive public—about 17%—knew three-fourths or more of the candidates' positions, whereas 56% of the general public knew one fourth or less of the positions.[10] Among the nonattentive public, a small minority on the low end of nonattention would be Hyman and Sheatsley's "chronic know-nothings," the "don't know" and "don't care" individuals alien to—and probably alienated from—the political arena.[11]

Observations of these knowledge levels also demonstrate the differences noted earlier between knowledge of things and knowledge about things. For the diffusion of news events, knowledge is measured more often than not in terms of simple awareness. This awareness of events and political actors (e.g., who are the candidates for governor) underscores the influence of the mass media in influencing salience, or knowledge *of* things, issues, and events. Studies that have investigated in greater depth the kinds of information held by individuals reveal that the more attentive public also acquires knowledge *about* things, issues, and events. Better informed voters, for example, are able to identify the major issues in an election and to discriminate among candidates' positions on issues.[12]

The attentive public on science and technology demonstrated understanding of such concepts as a "scientific study," "DNA," "radiation," and "molecule." It was able to discuss various sides to salient science and

---

[8]Almond, G. (1960). *The American people and foreign policy*. New York: Praeger.

[9]Miller, J. (1983). *The American people and science policy*. New York: Pergamon Press.

[10]Patterson, T. (1980). *The mass media election: How Americans choose their president*. New York: Praeger.

[11]Hyman, H., & Sheatsley, P. (1947). Some reasons why information campaigns fail. *Public Opinion Quarterly, 11*, 413–423.

[12]Patterson, op. cit.

technology issues; and it was able to discriminate among potential policy options.[13]

There also are variations in the rate at which information is acquired. The knowledge-gap hypothesis asserts that those who are better educated will acquire information at a faster rate than those with less education, resulting in a greater gap between the information haves and have-nots. In short, simply increasing the availability of information to the public at large is inadequate for the creation of informed public opinion.[14]

What are some of the factors that constrain the acquisition of information and the creation of informed public opinion? This chapter reviews two important mediators, formal education and media accessibility, diversity, and content. Chapter 9, which discusses participation in public affairs, reviews the nexus of individual characteristics, such as interests, motivations, and resources, that explain information-seeking patterns.

EDUCATION

Educational institutions are among the most important political socializers in our society. They are influential in shaping political—and other social and cultural—beliefs, attitudes, and values; in raising knowledge levels about government and politics; and in teaching the skills necessary for lifelong learning. Some scholars suggest that schools are even more influential in the political socialization of children aged 5–13 than the family.[15]

Numerous studies also have demonstrated the strong positive relationship between education, usually measured in terms of years of schooling, and levels of knowledge. Education also stimulates media use that, in turn, helps to account for greater information gains. These summary observations illustrate the important role that education plays:

> . . . research indicates that the extent of the audience member's exposure to formal education is the most powerful factor intervening between media usage and information level. (p. 75)[16]

When research is conducted using the traditional communication model, the results consistently show that those with less education and lower incomes

---

[13]Miller, op. cit.

[14]Tichenor, P. J., Donohue, G. A., & Olien, C. N. (in press). Knowledge gap research in retrospect. In J. G. Stappers (Ed.), *Approaches to mass communication.* Newbury Park, CA: Sage. Also see Tichenor, Donohue, & Olien, op. cit. and Severin & Tankard, op. cit.

[15]Hess, R. D., & Torney, J. V. (1967). *The development of political attitudes in children.* Chicago: Aldine.

[16]Robinson, J. (1972). Mass communication and information diffusion. In F. G. Kline & P. J. Tichenor (Eds.), *Current perspectives in mass communication research* (pp. 71–94). Beverly Hills: Sage.

are less likely to be information-seekers, use expert information sources, be informed generally. (p. 16)[17]

Education, again in tandem with media use, also plays a role in the capacity to actually have opinions. One study compared those who "don't know" versus those who have no opinion. The former might be termed *indifferent neutrals*, whereas the latter describes *true neutrals*, those who are informed, but are ambivalent or undecided. Those who said they did not know used the mass media to a lesser degree, were generally less knowledgeable, and had significantly less education.[18]

In terms of knowledge and information-seeking patterns, it is clear that education (a) supplies an information base that has an important input into the formation of beliefs, attitudes, and values; (b) teaches the value of being informed; and (c) teaches the skills necessary for information seeking and information processing behaviors. The other side of the coin, naturally, is that a lack of education serves as a constraint on all three.

MEDIA

What good is information if it is inaccessible to the individuals who need it? The notion of access implies the possibility of restraints. Lippmann described access in the context of censorship and propaganda:

> Without some form of censorship, propaganda in the strict sense of the word is impossible. In order to conduct a propaganda there must be some barrier between the public and the event. Access to the real environment must be limited, before anyone can create a pseudo-environment that he thinks wise or desirable. (p. 43)[19]

The literature on national development brings home quite clearly the issue of access to information and its intimate relationship to knowledge. Daniel Lerner's concept of the traditional personality, personified so poignantly in the Turkish peasant, illustrates how the inaccessibility of the mass media results in the consequent inability of the peasant to put himself in the shoes of the president. Asked by an interviewer what he would do if he were

---

[17]Dervin, B. (1980). Communication gaps and inequities: Moving toward a reconceptualization. In B. Dervin & M. J. Voigt (Eds.), *Progress in communication sciences* (Vol. 2, pp. 73–112). Norwood, NJ: Ablex.

[18]Faulkenberry, G. D., & Mason, R. (1978). Characteristics of nonopinion and no opinion response groups. *Public Opinion Quarterly, 42,* 533–543.

[19]Lippmann, W. (1922). *Public opinion.* New York: Macmillan.

president of Turkey, the peasant declared: "My God! How can you ask such a thing?" Lacking the skill of *empathy* so crucial in modern and complex societies, this tradition-minded peasant could not conceive of living anywhere else, much less of being someone else.[20] Lacking access to the mass media, these individuals lived in physical and psychological isolation.

Even in a society as media rich as the United States, the issue of access to mass communication remains a concern. For reasons as varied as geography and socioeconomic characteristics, some individuals have greater access to news media than others. In an information society that underscores even more the truism that information is power, the concern has frequently been voiced that disadvantaged groups become even more disadvantaged with the inaccessibility of new information technologies—the knowledge-gap problem.

Access is also underlined in the regulatory phrases of broadcasting "in the public interest, convenience and necessity." It is invoked in the notion of "the public's right to know." It was spelled out by the Commission on Freedom of the Press' admonition that the public be provided "full access to the day's intelligence."[21]

All of these notions about access suggest that people cannot begin to know unless they have access to the diversity of information that needs to be known. The premise for maintaining diversity of information sources has its roots in the philosophical notion that "truth will out" in the "free marketplace of ideas."[22] This philosophy is often relied on in debates about media ownership and in discussions about regulatory rationales, particularly for the broadcast media or for cross-media ownership issues.

Although the evidence regarding ownership patterns and their effects on media content appears mixed,[23] there is some evidence that, at the societal level, diversity of knowledge is correlated with the diversity of news sources available. For example, the diversity in the public's agenda of issues is correlated with media diversity in a community.[24] Diversity in this case was measured in terms of the number of problems mentioned when asked what is the most important problem facing the respondent's community or the nation.

---

[20]Lerner, D. (1958). *The passing of traditional society: Modernizing the Middle East.* Glencoe, IL: The Free Press.

[21]Hutchins, R. (1947). *Commission on freedom of the press: A free and responsible press.* Chicago: University of Chicago Press.

[22]Mill, J. S. (1972). On liberty. In J. S. Mill (Ed.), *Utilitarianism, On liberty, and considerations on representative government* (pp. 111–112). London: J. M. Dent.

[23]Picard, R. G. *et al.* (Eds.). (1988). *Press concentration and monopoly: New perspectives on newspaper ownership and operation.* Norwood, NJ: Ablex.

[24]Chaffee, S., & Wilson, D. (1977). Media rich, media poor: Two studies of diversity in agenda-holding. *Journalism Quarterly, 54,* 466–476.

MEDIA CONTENT

What we know about public affairs is further limited or enhanced by how the media cover public affairs. What we know is essentially a function of what we are exposed to and what we are not exposed to. Our lack of knowledge (or the lack of salience of other issues), particularly for those topics that we have little or no experience with, is in large part a function of what is *not* in the media.

One example of the potential impact of media content on public perceptions and knowledge is found in Lang and Lang's examination of the patterns of media coverage on Watergate.[25] Prior to the election, they found a lack of consistent coverage and a portrayal of an event, a burglary, rather than the portrayal of an issue.

Within 2 years, however, the President left the White House in disgrace. How did Watergate change from a narrow event to an issue of compelling proportions? The process had three elements: First, certain events were highlighted, drawing people's attention and creating discussion. Second, the media framed events in some context. What did the events mean? Was there any reason for concern? Third, the media linked the specific events of Watergate to more general political symbols.

All these factors suggest that the amount and the kind of information presented on Watergate had consequences for public knowledge and even for the subsequent behavior of Congress and President Nixon.[26]

CONCLUSION

In this chapter, we have discussed knowledge of public affairs as one of the constraints on social reality. There is evidence that knowledge of public affairs is generally not as high as we would ideally like it to be, although it is also unrealistic to expect everyone to be as well informed to the same degree.

Democracies have functioned fairly well with a highly knowledgeable and attentive few and a much larger group of citizens who are less knowledgeable, less interested, and less politically active.

The levels of knowledge generally achieved are further constrained or differentially enhanced by a number of factors. One of these is education,

[25]Lang, K., & Lang, G. E. (1981). Watergate: An exploration of the agenda-building process. In G. C. Wilhoit & H. de Bock (Eds.), *Mass communications yearbook 2* (pp. 447–468). Beverly Hills: Sage.

[26]Lang, G. E., & Lang, K. (1983). *The battle for public opinion.* New York: Columbia University Press.

which adds to one's store of information, enhances skills in knowledge acquisition, and develops interest in a wider variety of information.

In terms of media effects on knowledge, further constraints are imposed by accessibility, diversity, and content. Each of these exercises its own limiting effects on the knowledge-building process.

CHAPTER EIGHT

Forming Images and Opinions

Anyone who has read the letters to the editor section of a newspaper or magazine no doubt has been struck by the range of reactions evoked by the same article or public issue. This is hardly unusual, for our individual constellations of images and opinions act as unique filters through which each of us idiosyncratically processes our experiences. These personal filters act as screens that help us manage the daily barrage of information, provide defenses for our vulnerabilities, and allow us to express ourselves in ways that define our uniqueness to others.

In this chapter, we examine the interaction between all the "pictures in our heads" and the media's role in contributing to and elaborating on these pictures. The assumption here is that images are general concepts, which consist of a number of beliefs, or "facts," and opinions.[1]

---

[1]There is little consensus on using the terms *attitudes* and *opinions*. See, for example, Oskamp, S. (1977). *Attitudes and opinions*. Englewood Cliffs, NJ: Prentice-Hall; and McGuire, W. (1969). Attitudes and attitude change. In G. Lindzey & E. Aronson (Eds.), *Handbook of social psychology* (2nd ed., pp. 136–314). Reading, MA: Addison-Wesley. Some use attitudes more generically and regard opinions as a subset of attitudes; others argue that attitudes are affective, whereas opinions are "beliefs." It is certainly true that in terms of everyday usage, we often use these terms interchangeably. For example, we do not distinguish between the questions, "What is your opinion on nuclear power?" and "What are your attitudes toward nuclear power?" Either question may elicit responses dealing with our favoring or opposing nuclear power or whether we think it is a viable energy source. This is simply to recognize that such a debate exists. However, exploring this question is beyond the purposes of this chapter.

John Dewey observed that opinions arise out of perceptions of issues or problems and that the existence of those opinions engage people beyond the few who may be directly affected by an issue:

> [there is] the objective fact that human acts have consequences upon others, that some of these consequences are perceived, and that their perception leads to subsequent effort to control action so as to secure some consequences and avoid others. . . . The consequences are of two kinds, those which affect the persons directly engaged in a transaction, and those which affect others beyond those immediately concerned. (p. 12)[2]

Opinions are based on beliefs about the world around us. They may concern beliefs about perceived problems, about events, about other people. Our beliefs are our assumptions about what is factually true, about what the situation is, in regard to some aspect of our environment. The opinions that we form can be described along several dimensions:

- Direction, our feeling of being in favor of or opposed to something;
- Degree, how much we feel for or against something; ranging, for example, from slightly in favor to strongly in favor;
- Intensity, or depth of feeling; the intensity of opinions regarding a brand of breakfast cereal most likely is quite different from the intensity of feelings about the abortion issue;
- Salience, the prominence or centrality in our minds and lives of the object or topic about which we have an opinion.

In many instances, opinions tend to be ephemeral, rising and falling as the things we think about blossom and fade from our consciousness, dominating, then falling away from, our conversations with others. In other instances, opinions can be fairly stable. For example, our opinions about the presidency may not change much over time, whereas our opinions about specific presidents may vacillate with their changing fortunes.

DEVELOPMENT OF PUBLIC OPINION

How does public opinion develop? First, as Dewey pointed out, a "private conflict" has to be publicized in order to be recognized beyond those directly affected. Sometimes, individuals or groups exert major effort to gain publicity for an issue in which they have a personal stake. In doing so, they hope to shape the contours of the issue according to their own interests. Note the intensive lobbying over the past decade between two positions

---

[2]Dewey, J. (1927). *The public and its problems.* Chicago: Swallow Press.

on the abortion issue: "freedom of choice" versus "right to life." Even the name of an issue can make a difference!

Once an issue gains the spotlight, people start discussing the topic, and in some instances, they may seek more information about it or try to do something about the problem, particularly when it is something personally relevant. It is during this activation phase that individuals informally "sample" others' opinions and evaluate the validity of their own opinions. It was James Madison who observed rather astutely:

> If it be true that all governments rest on opinion, it is no less true that the strength of opinion in each individual, and its practical influence on his conduct, depends much on the number which he supposes to have entertained the same opinion. The reason of man, like man himself, is timid and cautious when left alone, and acquires firmness and confidence in proportion to the number with which it is associated. (p. 329)[3]

A recent theory of public opinion, known as the "spiral of silence," builds on Madison's observations that people's confidence in their opinions is increased if they think others agree with them. Advanced in the early 1970s by a prominent German public opinion researcher, Elisabeth Noelle-Neumann, the spiral of silence theory predicts that people will be more likely to publicly state their opinions if they believe their opinions are in the majority or are becoming more widespread.[4] Likewise, because of a fear of isolation, they will be less likely to expose their opinions publicly if they feel that their opinions are losing ground. Because those who perceive their opinions to be dominant or on the rise are more willing to speak out, and those who sense that their opinions are in the minority or on the decline are more likely to be silent, this results in a "spiralling process which increasingly establishes one opinion as the prevailing one" (p. 44).[5] Of course, this is not universally the case because not everyone accurately perceives the trend in public opinion. There is a tendency among some individuals to project their own opinions onto others. This has been called the *looking glass phenomenon*. Its complement is *pluralistic ignorance*, a tendency not to know at all what opinions others hold. Both tendencies, of course, limit the likelihood that a spiral of silence will occur.[6]

Support for this theory has been mixed. People do not necessarily become silent if they think they hold a minority opinion, especially if they are

[3]Madison, J. (1937). *The federalist*. New York: The Modern Library.

[4]Noelle-Neumann, E. (1984). *The spiral of silence*. Chicago: University of Chicago Press.

[5]Noelle-Neumann, E. (1974). The spiral of silence: A theory of public opinion. *Journal of Communication, 24*, 43–51.

[6]Price, V., & Roberts, D. (1987). Public opinion processes. In C. R. Burger & S. H. Chaffee (Eds.), *Handbook of communication science* (pp. 781–816). Newbury Park, CA: Sage.

supported by their own reference groups. Some people even use their own opinions as a basis for estimating the overall climate of opinion. It is likely, too, that willingness to voice an opinion depends on the kind of issue being considered. The spiral of silence theory is more likely to hold for issues involving personal or sensitive information than for other kinds of issues.[7] Although a spiral of silence does not always occur in the development of public opinion on an issue, nevertheless, the point is well taken that people do regularly scan their environment in order to orient themselves to the current situation.[8]

FUNCTIONS OF OPINIONS

"Of what use to a man are his opinions?" This was the question raised in the classic study by Harvard psychologists about the relationship between personality and opinions.[9] A functional approach to the study of opinions suggests that opinions fulfill basic personality needs. The typology advanced by psychologist Daniel Katz suggests a number of needs that can be fulfilled by holding opinions.[10]

1. *Instrumental or utilitarian function.* This arises from the assumption that people are always engaged in the minimization of pain and the maximization of pleasure. In many situations, people shape their responses according to this pleasure–pain principle. For example, holding an opinion antithetical to the principle of academic freedom can be difficult in an academic environment because of strong peer disapproval. An individual who subscribes to the principle of equity in the workplace may soon feel guilt and discomfort when a male friend gets promoted over a more qualified female.

2. *The ego-defensive function.* The ego, one's self-concept, is vulnerable to many threats. Our opinions sometimes are used as defense mechanisms. When a person is unable to admit certain feelings about him or herself, one possible defense mechanism is to project those feelings onto another person or group. Although utilitarian attitudes are based on the reference object,

---

[7]Salmon, C. T., & Kline, F. G. (1985). The spiral of silence ten years later: An examination and evaluation. In K. R. Sanders, L. L. Kaid, & D. Nimmo (Eds.), *Political communication yearbook 1984* (pp. 3–30). Carbondale: Southern Illinois University Press.

[8]McCombs, M., & Weaver, D. (1985). Toward a merger of gratifications and agenda-setting research. In K. E. Rosengren, L. A. Wenner, & P. Palmgren (Eds.), *Media gratifications research* (pp. 95–108). Beverly Hills: Sage.

[9]Smith, M. B., Bruner, J. S., & White, R. W. (1956). *Opinions and personality.* New York: Wiley.

[10]Katz, D. (1960). The functional approach to the study of attitudes. *Public Opinion Quarterly, 24,* 163–204.

in the case of ego-defensive attitudes, the reference object or group is simply a convenient target.

3. *Value-expression function*. There are aspects of our personality that need elaboration, and values—those overarching belief systems—are among these. If a woman prides herself as being a feminist, she will most likely maintain "feminist" opinions on a wide variety of issues—affirmative action, pay equity, the elimination of all-male clubs, and so forth.

4. *Knowledge function*. One of the enduring motives found in numerous audience surveys on media use is "to keep up with what's going on in the world." Opinions play an important role in providing closure as one sorts through the volume and complexities of the daily information barrage. Having arrived at an opinion implies that a conclusion has been reached after satisfying a need to know; it implies rationality on the part of the individual.

Of course, new information that is incongruent with opinions already held can cause discomfort. Not only is incoming information filtered and processed; it is shaped to conform to the existing belief patterns to be logical and consistent.[11]

There are other reasons beyond psychological ones that explain the need for opinion holding. As pointed out earlier, reference groups—any group or organization with whom a person strongly identifies—play an important role in people's lives, and these reference groups influence both holding opinions and the direction of those opinions. One cannot truly support gun control and be a member of the National Rifle Association, nor is it easy to simultaneously be sympathetic to labor organizations and support management efforts to decertify unions. Even if one's own union is not on strike, crossing a picket line would be inconsistent for a union member.

Can opinions change? In some instances, opinions are virtually fixed and unmovable. This is true of those opinions that are tied to central values and core beliefs. In many other instances, opinions are rather fluid. They can change because the problem that brought them about in the first place has been resolved or has changed. They also can shift because new information has restructured our perspective.

Pictures of the world exist in our heads. They are there as products of socialization, of education, and of incidental learning from both mass communication and personal experience. A variety of terms have been utilized to describe these images. Lippmann, for example, used the term *stereotypes* to describe our stock of mental images:

---

[11]Festinger, L. (1957). *A theory of cognitive dissonance*. Stanford: Stanford University Press. (See especially pp. 123–176.)

[Stereotypes] are an ordered, more or less consistent picture of the world, to which our habits, our tastes, our capacities, our comforts and our hopes have adjusted themselves. They may not be a complete picture of the world, but they are a picture of a possible world to which we are adapted. In that world, people and things have their well known places, and do certain expected things. We feel at home there. (p. 24)[12]

Social psychologists use the more neutral term *schemas*, which performs in a similar manner as stereotypes. Schemas denote knowledge structures based on experience that organize people's perceptions of the world.[13] The analytical approach to schemas is based on the notion that people are "cognitive misers," that is, people have well-defined cognitive limits.[14] Their attention spans are short in duration and narrowly focused, and the range of their active memory processing is short.

In addition to economy of effort, however, is the notion of images as defense. It is behind these walls of imagery where, Lippmann maintained, "we can continue to feel ourselves safe in the position we occupy" (p. 96).[15]

IMAGES VERSUS ISSUES

The images-versus-issues debate about what influences a voter's choice at the polls has particularly intrigued political scientists since Donald Stokes' classic analysis of American elections.[16] His study demonstrated that the emergence of a particularly attractive candidate resulted in voters switching allegiance to him, whereas a particularly unattractive candidate drove party supporters away. In short, images were influential. Even in presidential debates where there had been considerable focus on issues, viewers were more likely to remember attributes relating to competence or performance than to remember issue-related information.[17] Doris Graber also found the public more likely to extract image-related than issue-related information about the president from general press coverage.[18]

---

[12]Lippmann, W. (1922). *Public opinion.* New York: Macmillan.

[13]Lau, R. (1986). Political schemata, candidate evaluations, and voting behavior. In R. Lau & D. Sears (Eds.), *Political cognition.* Hillsdale, NJ: Lawrence Erlbaum Associates.

[14]Taylor, S. E. (1981). The interface of cognitive and social psychology. In J. Harvey (Ed.), *Cognition, social behavior, and the environment* (pp. 189–213). Hillsdale, NJ: Lawrence Erlbaum Associates.

[15]Lippmann, op. cit., p. 96.

[16]Stokes, D. E. (1966). Some dynamic elements of contests for the presidency. *American Political Science Review, 60,* 19–28.

[17]Miller, A. H., & Miller, W. E. (1976). Ideology in the 1972 election: Myth or reality. *American Political Science Review, 70,* 832–849.

[18]Graber, D. (1988). *Processing the news* (2nd ed.). New York: Longman.

Even more interesting were the results from a reanalysis of responses to an open-ended question about voters' likes and dislikes concerning the two major party presidential candidates. Data covering national elections from 1952 through 1984 showed that personal attributes had as large or a larger impact than policies on the presidential vote in five out of seven elections. More surprising was the finding that even among the better educated, these images based on personal attributes exerted a significant effect on voting.[19]

MEDIA IMPACT ON IMAGES

Do the news media influence this concentration on image attributes? There is increasing evidence that indeed the news media, and especially television, play an important role in this area. One year-long election study found that the media play a major role in making some candidates, and certain of their attributes, more prominent than others.[20] In fact, this kind of media coverage probably has more influence on voters' early perceptions of the campaign, and the final choices available at election time, than does news coverage of issues. Prior knowledge, high interest, and frequent media use were all correlated with learning about the personality traits and campaign styles of the candidates. In the early primary elections, especially, those candidates who received the most media coverage were likely to become the most well-known, and those characteristics of candidates that were most heavily emphasized in the news media were most likely to be cited in voters' descriptions of the candidates.

In addition, voters thought it was easier to learn about candidate images than about issues, especially the personality traits and styles of the candidates rather than their job qualifications and political views. It seems likely that most voters, with limited time to devote to thinking about elections, still find it easier to learn about the personalities and styles of candidates than about complicated issue positions, especially if these voters rely on television for most of their information about an election.

The format of television news lends itself to this influential role. As Doris Graber observed:

> The skimpiness of television issue coverage, particularly the dearth of quotes by candidates, meant that people who relied primarily on television for campaign information learned little about the candidates' stands on issues and even less about the candidates' priorities. This left the television viewer with

[19]Glass, D. P. (1985). Evaluating presidential candidates: Who focuses on their personal attributes? *Public Opinion Quarterly, 49,* 517–34.

[20]Weaver, D. H., Graber, D. A., McCombs, M. E., & Eyal, C. H. (1981). *Media agenda-setting in a presidential election: Issues, images, and interest.* New York: Praeger. (See especially pp. 162–193 on images.)

information weighted heavily in favor of using characteristics of the man, rather than issue positions, as voting criteria. (pp. 300–301)[21]

On the other hand, the media are not entirely at fault for this dearth of issue information. In order to please large and diverse audiences, candidates' issue positions quite often remain ambiguous during a campaign, allowing more weight to the potential influence of image information supplied by the media and providing the individual more latitude to fill in the blanks.

Images of the presidency also revolve around such personal attributes as "competence," "leadership," "integrity," and "empathy." Evaluations of particular presidents on these attributes are, of course, grounded in real events and earned reputations, but as portrayed in the mass media.[22] Even before they get to be president, presidential candidates' images are shaped by media portrayals of their "viability," or their likelihood of being nominated, and their "electability" as president.

For example, almost 66% of the network news coverage during the 1980 elections was of the "horse-race" variety, which reports little more than who's ahead.[23] Just as significant, while judgments of competence or integrity typically are provided by the candidates, their opponents or their staff in general elections, horse-race topics are virtually the only ones on which reporters offer their own evaluative judgments.[24]

The language used by the media also provides important raw material for image construction. As Edelman maintained,

> It is language about political events, not the events in any other sense, that people experience; even developments that are close by take their meaning from the language that depicts them. (p. 104)[25]

The emotional symbolism aroused by such labels as "terrorist," or "freedom fighter," or the perception of a problem cast as a "national security" problem versus one under the guise of "the people's right to know" suggests the volatility that can erupt when stimulus meets individual schema. Language and images in the media can be especially influential in the area

---

[21]Graber, D. (1976). Press and TV as opinion resources in presidential campaigns. *Public Opinion Quarterly, 40*, 285–303.

[22]Kinder, D. (1986). Presidential character revisited: In R. Lau & D. Sears (Eds.), *Political cognition*. Hillsdale, NJ: Lawrence Erlbaum Associates.

[23]Robinson, M. J., & Sheehan, M. A. (1983). *Over the wire and on TV: CBS and UPI in campaign '80*. New York: Russell Sage. Also see Buchanan, op. cit., chapter 4 for details on the 1988 election.

[24]Semetko, H. A., Blumler, J. G., Gurevitch, M., & Weaver, D. H. (1991). *The formation of campaign agendas*. Hillsdale, NJ: Lawrence Erlbaum Associates.

[25]Edelman, M. (1988). *Constructing the political spectacle*. Chicago: University of Chicago Press.

of foreign affairs where there is little personal experience to draw from. This is well illustrated in David Altheide's case study of the Iranian hostage crisis, where the news coverage focused almost exclusively on mobs and demonstrations regardless of the day's news.[26]

Another area where the media contribute to images is expectations. In reporting the risks associated with various technologies, anything from nuclear power to birth control devices, the media establish a framework of expectations by (a) making risks visible; (b) providing a context for evaluating these risks, and (c) shaping expectations about similar or related risks.[27] Women's images of birth-control approaches and their subsequent behavior changes, for example, correlated significantly with reports in the news linking the use of contraceptives to the risk of strokes, problems with IUD devices, and the like.[28]

IMAGES AND OPINION FORMATION

Why should images play such a significant role in information processing and opinion formation? Balance theorists such as Heider have maintained that one way people manage information is by keeping some anchor in reference points and evaluating other attitude objects in comparison with the main anchor.[29] Because the president plays such a dominant role in our political landscape, judgments in national politics can often be simplified in relation to the individual's perceptions of the president's traits and intentions.

The reliance on personal traits that characterize images also arises from the social settings with which we are more intimately familiar—that of interpersonal relationships. As Lane suggested, "People seek in leaders the same qualities they seek in friends, that is, they simply generalize their demands from one case to the other" (p. 447).[30]

Finally, images provide a psychological security blanket. In his excellent analysis of the use of political symbolism in politics, Edelman argued that symbols are short-hand means of evoking appropriate stereotypic images on the part of the perceiver, allowing the latter the security that the world

---

[26]Altheide, D. (1986). *Media power*. Beverly Hills: Sage.

See also Altheide, D. (1981). Iran vs. TV news: The hostage story out of context. In W. C. Adams (Ed.), *Television coverage of the Middle East* (pp. 128–157). Norwood, NJ: Ablex.

[27]Nelkin, D. (1989). Communicating technological risk: The social construction of risk perception. *Annual Review of Public Health, 10*, 95–113.

[28]Jones, E., Beniger, J., & Westoff, C. (1980). Pill and IUD discontinuation in the U.S., 1970–1975: Influence of the media. *Family Planning Perspective, 12*, 293–300.

[29]Heider, F. (1958). *The psychology of interpersonal relations*. New York: Wiley.

[30]Lane, R. (1978). Interpersonal relations and leadership in a "cold society." *Comparative Politics, 10*, 443–59.

out there is organized, just, and good.[31] For a long time, the Berlin Wall symbolized the political and ideological divisions between east and west, communist and democratic systems, and military alliances that grew out of World War II. The breaking down of this wall—in political, physical and psychological terms—was the breaking down of such a long-held and powerful stereotypic image that for weeks thereafter, there was as much disbelief, uncertainty, and anxiety as there was celebration. "Is It Possible?" *Newsweek* magazine (Nov. 20, 1989) asked in its cover story.

If images and opinions are central to an individual's mental set and ability to function well, does this mean that selective exposure—the active attempt to seek out complementary information and avoid that which is discrepant— becomes a natural part of every individual's coping behaviors? Selective exposure assumes deliberate attention to carefully selected messages and indeed, there is some evidence, given the sheer volume of sources, delivery channels, or topics available, that this occurs in certain instances.[32]

On the other hand, a number of factors moderate the amount of selective exposure engaged in by most people and heighten the potential influence of external sources such as the news media. First, the format and content of mass communication is designed to draw an audience's attention. The use of headlines, graphics, visuals, music, even scent, as some perfume advertisers are now doing, are ways of "packaging" messages for maximum attention. Second, there is a certain amount of passivity on the part of most individuals, given such things as time constraints and lack of familiarity with most issues being covered for the first time. And, finally, there is the sheer ubiquity of mass communication.

Although the evidence for selective exposure is relatively weak, there is more support for selective *perception* and selective *interpretation* of political information.[33] By paying attention to certain points in messages and by interpreting facts differently, people can maintain strongly held beliefs and opinions without seeming to be inconsistent and without feeling any psychological discomfort or dissonance. Neuman argued that some of the clearest examples of selective perception come from the research on political debates, where voters consistently interpret their own favorite candidate as having "won" the debate. Whereas there is considerable evidence for selective perception and interpretation, the studies on selective *retention*, or recall, show that this effect does not seem to be terribly strong.[34]

[31]Edelman, M. (1964). *The symbolic uses of politics.* Urbana, IL: University of Illinois Press.

[32]Zillmann, D., & Bryant, J. (1985). *Selective exposure to communications.* Hillsdale, NJ: Lawrence Erlbaum Associates.

[33]Neuman, W. R. (1986). *The paradox of mass politics.* Cambridge, MA: Harvard University Press.

[34]Neuman, op. cit., pp. 153–154.

In summary, when we look at how an individual processes information and formulates new opinions and images (or reshapes those already held), we have a transactional situation where images and opinions can be shaped by external sources, but are also created and used by the individual to help manage his or her ability to function in the social world.

CHAPTER NINE

Participation in Public Affairs

If participation in public affairs really is a prerequisite to the functioning of democratic systems, it is amazing that such systems have survived for so long and so successfully. The truth is that our political system has endured in spite of, and perhaps even because of, the lack of active participation of many of its citizenry. To obtain full participation from every single individual would simply be chaos.

The first axiom of political participation is that although we adhere in theory to the notion that participation in public affairs is a virtue, political reality has consistently demonstrated the opposite. There always have been large individual differences in participatory activity. The second axiom is that this participation also varies widely according to time, issue, or place—those who actively participate on one issue may be apathetic on another.

LEVELS OF PARTICIPATION

Political scientists have focused considerable attention on political activity, arriving at a variety of categories that reflect differences in attention to politics, potential for action, or type of activity. For example, as we saw in chapter 7, the public has sometimes been subdivided into those who pay attention and those who do not (the "attentives" vs. the "nonattentives"); those who can be moved to political action and those less so (the "mobilizable" vs. the "nonmobilizable"); or those whose range of political activity varies from nonvoting to simple voting to more active levels of participation, such as working for political parties, contacting public officials, demonstrating, and so forth. One political scientist, Lester Milbrath, has metaphorically described these categories in terms of a Roman gladiatorial contest: the "gladiators" who actually do battle; the "spectators" who cheer, jeer, and finally decide on the victor; and the "apathetics," or those who don't even watch the spectacle.[1]

Although voting is perhaps the most obvious political activity and one that much research attention has focused on, there is a wide range of activities that can be called *political participation*. Lehnen has identified three types of behaviors that constitute day-to-day political activities: support, evaluation, and political action.[2]

Supportive activities are those that have the effect of maintaining the political system, the symbolic activities that constitute the "political glue" for the system. For example, these include paying heed to such "good citizen" mandates as paying one's taxes, obeying laws, or supporting the tenets in the Bill of Rights.

Evaluative behavior, according to Lehnen, can be subdivided into two major opinion processes: opinion formation and the development of political judgments.[3] The former involves an examination of saliency, or whether citizens are aware of activities of political elites and the important issues of the day. The second relates to favorable or unfavorable opinions about the issues, how such evaluations are made, whether and how they change.

The third type of behavior—political action—is easily identified and measured. How often do people contact government officials? Do they write letters to the editor? Do they talk politics with others? Sign petitions? Call a phone-in program to express an opinion? As one scholar put it, "A substantial number of people vote but participate no further in politics, while almost everyone who is active in political campaigning and fund raising votes" (p. 85).[4]

FACTORS AFFECTING PARTICIPATION

Participation can be influenced by many different individual, institutional, and environmental or situational factors. Individual factors include such

---

[1]Milbrath, L. (1965). *Political participation*. Chicago: Rand McNally. See also Milbrath (1981). Political participation. In S. Long (Ed.), *The handbook of political behavior* (pp. 57–61). New York: Plenum Press.

[2]Lehnen, R. G. (1976). *American institutions, political opinion, and public policy*. Chicago: Dryden Press.

[3]Ibid., 15–18.

[4]Neuman, W. R. (1986). *The paradox of mass politics*. Cambridge, MA: Harvard University Press.

background elements as family influence, group influence, education, and the like. Verba and Nie, for example, suggested a social-status theory of participation, postulating that an individual's class and educational background provide both the skills and opportunities to participate.[5]

Education has been a consistent predictor of participation. It provides exposure to a wider range of ideas, hones analytical and information-gathering skills, and transmits values that enhance citizenship. On an informal level, family socialization patterns also influence participatory behavior. For example, growing up in a "media-rich" environment where open communication among family members is valued also increases the likelihood of regular attention to news content or the ease with which one expresses an opinion.[6] Studies of newspaper subscribing have demonstrated that having a newspaper in the home as a child is a good predictor of future newspaper subscribing.[7] All these factors contribute to political sophistication and, as one political scientist put it:

> The fact of the matter is that political sophistication is strongly correlated with political activity. The better informed are more likely to vote and more likely to participate in politics beyond the act of voting. (p. 85)[8]

One's reference groups also play an important role in political participation. The empirical finding by Campbell and his associates that "nonvoting, as well as the direction of voting, tends to be shared behavior" (p. 9) has been documented time and again.[9] Indeed, one can say that reference groups (or the lack of them) play a large part in determining the type and the amount of information one has, one's beliefs and values, and the nature of one's behaviors.

Even such a nebulous group as the perceived majority and its position on any given issue has been demonstrated at times to exert influence on one's opinion and one's willingness to express an opinion. This tendency, known as the "spiral of silence," was discussed more fully in chapter 8.[10]

Environmental and institutional opportunities also affect how much or whether one participates. At various times, certain groups have been dis-

---

[5]Verba, S., & Nie, N. H. (1972). *Participation in America: Political democracy and social equality.* New York: Harper.

[6]Chaffee, S. H., McLeod, J. M., & Wackman, D. B. (1973). Family communication patterns and adolescent political participation. In J. Dennis (Ed.), *Socialization to politics* (pp. 349–364). New York: Wiley.

[7]Einsiedel, E. F. (1983, December 27). Comparisons of subscribers and non-subscribers. *ANPA News Research Report* (No. 39).

[8]Neuman, op. cit.

[9]Campbell, A., Converse, P., Miller, W., & Stokes, D. (1960). *The American voter.* New York: Wiley. See also Neuman, op. cit., pp. 126–127.

[10]Noelle-Neuman, E. (1974). The spiral of silence: A theory of public opinion. *Journal of Communications, 24*(2), 43–51.

enfranchised for extended periods of time. Blacks, for example, could not vote in some parts of the country for a long time. And even when they were finally given the right to vote, their participation rates remained lower than Whites, a fact attributed to the reality that having suddenly acquired the right to vote did not necessarily translate into using the opportunities right away. Having been used to a long history without this right, its exercise with its attendant self-confidence and information base was not going to happen overnight.

Incentives or disincentives to participate also determine participation. In Italy, for example, those who do not vote have their official documents stamped as "Failed to vote," which can create problems in future attempts to obtain other government papers. Not surprisingly, turnout remains extremely high, exceeding 90% regularly. In Poland, outlawing of the Solidarity party at one point effectively removed one avenue for political activity, at least overtly. In the United States where the burden of voter registration falls on the individual citizen, voting participation rates have lagged behind those countries where the government assumes the responsibility for registration.[11] Where a Canadian, for instance, has an enumerator come to his doorstep to register him, an American has to find the time and the proper place to register.

Situational factors also affect participation. In the case of elections, the interest generated among voters—determined by the clarity of choice among candidates, the importance to the voters of a proposition on the ballot, the interest generated by campaign propaganda—can influence voter turnout. In Louisiana, the election of a high-ranking official of the Ku Klux Klan who himself was repudiated by the Republican party under whose banner he was running, was attributed to what constituents saw as "outside interference." Even such factors as the weather or a candidate's resources to "bring out the vote" can have an impact. On the issue of the environment, the syndrome now commonly called NIMBY, or "not in my backyard" has created activists out of individuals over such issues as the location of a nuclear power plant or a toxic waste dump.

THE MEDIA AND PARTICIPATION

The mass media play an important role in defining the nature and extent of political participation. First, attentiveness to the news of the day can be considered a form of political participation. It is, in fact, probably the most common and widespread form of political participation. This "civic duty

---

[11]Lehnen, op. cit.

to be informed" is an important element in the array of obligations of a "good citizen."[12] If we examine other forms of political activity, there are a number of ways their extent and character have been shaped by the media. At the lowest level, the media provide the public with information that legitimates the system, a basis for a "reaffirmation of faith" that arises from the coverage of such mundane things as a trial being concluded ("justice has been carried out"), an election being conducted, a mechanism being set up to facilitate a labor dispute, and so forth.

It goes without saying that information questioning the legitimacy of a government is also often channelled via the mass media. The democratic movements all over Eastern Europe followed on the heels of the much publicized policies of *glasnost* and *perestroika*, which effectively allowed opposition voices to challenge and subsequently change the old order.

The mass media also provide opportunities for participation by highlighting specific problems pertinent to specific groups or individuals. In influencing the issue agenda of the day, not only do the media suggest areas of concern, but they also indicate what has been done to date to solve the problem and the alternative solutions proposed. In so doing, opportunities are presented to the citizen to decide to engage in political activity (or to choose otherwise). Gay communities in many parts of the country, and especially in San Francisco, were galvanized into action when they perceived that the federal government was not paying sufficient attention and committing inadequate resources to the AIDS problem.

Finally, the media provide illustrations of methods of participation. Protests during the Vietnam War took similar forms in various parts of the country, such as teach-ins and draft-card burnings. More recently, hunger strikes, hijackings, and sit-ins are in vogue. In their coverage of various forms of political behavior, the media provide a primer on the more effective forms of activity—as well as those less successful.

Lemert and his colleagues have used the term *mobilizing information* to describe information that allows people to act on existing attitudes.[13] Media coverage provides mobilizing information that might be "locational"—the time and place for an event to occur or the site of a particular problem; "identificational"—a name or physical description; or "tactical"— the modus operandi or behavioral models that have been used.

But what of the nonparticipants or the less active citizenry? Much of this chapter has been devoted to participation and the media's role in political activity, but we did start out by recognizing that the vast majority of the

---

[12]McCombs, M., & Poindexter, P. (1983). The duty to keep informed: News exposure and civic obligation. *Journal of Communication, 33,* 88–96.

[13]Lemert, J. B. (1981). *Does mass communication change public opinion after all?* Chicago: Nelson-Hall.

public remain spectators in the political arena, stay away entirely, or have too many distractions from the spectacle to pay more than passing notice.

Indeed, Lippmann maintained that it is the vicissitudes of daily living that command most people's energies and attention, and to expect the public to remain absorbed in political affairs would be unnatural.[14] There is considerable evidence to support his contention. Almond and Verba found that 25% of Americans admitted never discussing public affairs.[15] Hyman and Sheatsley found a group of chronic "know-nothings" on many public issues.[16] And more recently, an analysis of nine national voting studies from 1948 to 1980 found that "the public is profoundly uninterested in the political world" (p. 9).[17] Quite simply, interest in public affairs remains a limited commodity.

Time has also played an important role in the extent of participation. Consider, for example, how people attend to the media as a form of participation. During Lippmann's time, close to 66% of adults said they read two or three newspapers. Very few readers today would make such a claim. The difference, however, is not simply that citizens then were more civic-minded; not only are there fewer newspapers today (an urban area with two competing newspapers is, in fact, the exception today) but there has been a veritable explosion of new media in the last 60 years as well.

Political efficacy—or the lack of it—can also constrain political participation. When a national sample of adults was asked "How much do you think your opinion can count in influencing the actions and policies of the local government?", only 34% responded "some" or "a lot."[18] Those with a low sense of efficacy not only participate less, a fact that has been demonstrated in a variety of cross-cultural contexts, but they are also less attentive to the mass media, believe public officials are not responsive, and that the political process is too complex to be understood.[19] However, efficacy, like participation, is an attribute that is hardly widespread.

---

[14]Lippmann, W. (1922). *Public opinion*. New York: Macmillan.

[15]Almond, G. A., & Verba, S. (1963). *The civic culture*. Princeton: Princeton University Press.

[16]Hyman, H., & Sheatsley, P. (1947). Some reasons why information campaigns fail. *Public Opinion Quarterly, 11*, 412–423.

[17]Neuman, op. cit., p. 9.

[18]Newspaper Advertising Bureau. (1988). *News and newspaper reading habits: Results from a national survey*. Unpublished report.

[19]Almond & Verba, op. cit.

PART FIVE

Creating Public Opinion

CHAPTER TEN

The Transfer
of Interests

The mass media are not the only influence on the public and government agendas, although they are an important force. Other groups and institutions play significant roles in setting the public and policy agendas, often through influencing the media agenda. Increasingly, as political party identification in this country has declined, special interest groups have played a more important role in getting some issues onto the policy agenda of various government bodies (legislatures, agencies, courts, etc.),[1] often through influencing the media agenda as well as through direct lobbying of government officials.[2]

This chapter looks first at what we know about the influences on media agendas,[3] and second at the influences on government (policy) agen-

[1]Berry, J. M. (1984). *The interest group society*. Boston: Little, Brown.

[2]See Rogers, E. M., & Dearing, J. W. (1988). Agenda-setting research: Where has it been, where is it going? In J. A. Anderson (Ed.), *Communication yearbook 11* (pp. 555–594). Newbury Park, CA: Sage.

[3]See, for example, Weaver, D., & Elliott, S. N. (1985). Who sets the agenda for the media? A study of local agenda-building. *Journalism Quarterly, 62*, 87–94.

Lang, G., & Lang, K. (1982). Watergate: An exploration of the agenda-building process. In G. C. Wilhoit & H. de Bock (Eds.), *Mass communication review yearbook* (Vol. 2, pp. 447–468). Newbury Park, CA: Sage.

Gandy, O. (1982). *Beyond agenda setting: Information subsidies and public policy*. Norwood, NJ: Ablex.

Turk, J. V. (1986). Information subsidies and media content: A study of public relations influence on the news. *Journalism Monographs, 100*.

das.[4] This knowledge is also related to public opinion formation and change.

SETTING THE MEDIA AGENDA

If the media mainly pass on the agendas of other influential actors and institutions in society, it would not be quite accurate to refer to the media as *setting* agendas. Perhaps "amplifying" or "legitimizing" might be a more accurate description than "setting" agendas in such a case. But the evidence is mixed on how much discretion the media in this country do have in determining which issues will receive the most (and the least) attention.

A major year-long examination of the 1976 U.S. presidential election found that the issues the candidates stressed most prominently were not the same as those displayed most prominently in the news.[5] In their campaign speeches and televised political advertising, the candidates talked most about "diffuse" issues—broad policy proposals such as the commitment to maintaining a healthy economy. In contrast, the media tended to stress what have been called "clear-cut" issues—those that neatly divide the candidates, provoke conflict, and can be summarized with shorthand labels such as "busing" and "detente."[6]

Another study of the 1984 U.S. presidential campaign and the 1983 British general election found more discretion in the United States than in Britain for media agenda setting.[7] Although the correlations between media and candidate agendas in Britain were very strong, suggesting that the British media were closely reflecting the agendas of the candidates and parties, these correlations were much weaker in the United States, suggesting that newspaper and television journalists were exercising more of their own judgment about which issues were most and least important.

At the British Broadcasting Corporation (BBC), journalists voiced support for the principle that "politics belongs to the politicians," but at NBC in the United States there was more of a sense of a tug of war between politicians' and journalists' interests, including a need to ensure that the politicians did not get a "free publicity ride."

---

[4]Cobb, R. W., & Elder, C. D. (1983). *Participation in American politics: The dynamics of agenda-building* (2nd ed.). Baltimore, MD: John Hopkins University Press.

Nelson, B. J. (1984). *Making an issue of child abuse: Political agenda setting for social problems*. Chicago: University of Chicago Press.

[5]Patterson, T. (1980). *The media election: How Americans choose their president*. New York: Praeger. See also Asp, K. (1983). The struggle for the agenda: Party agenda, media agenda and voter agenda in the 1979 Swedish election campaign. *Communication Research, 10,* 333–356.

[6]Seymour-Ure, C. (1974). *The political impact of mass media*. Newbury Park, CA: Sage.

[7]Semetko, H. A., Blumler, J. G., Gurevitch, M., & Weaver, D. (1991). *The formation of campaign agendas*. Hillsdale, NJ: Lawrence Erlbaum Associates.

All this suggests that in recent U.S. presidential election campaigns, the media have exercised some independent agenda-setting power, although that power is constrained by what the candidates and their staffs say and do, by how much access is granted to journalists, and by which other news sources are available.

Many observers of journalists and politicians at the national and state level stress the dependence of journalists on government news sources, but most do not systematically compare the agendas of those news sources with subsequent media agendas.[8] One 1984 study that did compare agendas of Louisiana state agencies and eight daily newspapers in three Louisiana cities found some influence of government public information officers' calls, press conferences, documents, and news releases on the media agenda for about half of the stories written about these state agencies.[9] But this study also concluded that "daily newspaper reporters appear to be the primary decision-makers in terms of what is or is not included in newspaper content" (p. 25).[10]

Two studies on the influence of Richard Nixon's and Jimmy Carter's State of the Union addresses on the press agenda in 1970 and 1978 found that although the dominant influence on the media agenda is the ongoing stream of events shaped by the news values and practices of journalism, a major speech by the president can influence the subsequent media agenda.[11]

Taken together, these studies suggest some ability of journalists to set national and state agendas, but not an unlimited power. As the study of Louisiana state agencies noted, even when public relations sources do not contribute information to a news story, other types of sources also contribute information and increase the prominence of certain stories.[12] Responsible journalists neither make up stories nor ignore important tips from reliable news sources.

DETERMINING THE LOCAL AGENDA

The influence of government news sources on the media agenda varies not only by the type of story being covered, but also by the level of govern-

---

[8]See, for example, Sigal, L. V. (1973). *Reporters and officials*. Lexington, MA: D. C. Heath.
Dunn, D. D. (1969). *Public officials and the press*. Reading, MA: Addison-Wesley.
Hess, S. (1984). *The government/press connection*. Washington, DC: The Brookings Institution.

[9]Turk, op. cit.

[10]Turk, op. cit., p. 25.

[11]Wanta, W., Stephenson, M. A., Turk, J. V., & McCombs, M. (1989). How president's state of union talk influenced news media agendas. *Journalism Quarterly, 66*, 537–541.
Gilberg, S., Eyal, C., McCombs, M., & Nicholas, D. (1980). The state of the union address and the press agenda. *Journalism Quarterly, 57*, 584–588.

[12]Turk, op. cit., pp. 27–28.

ment. Whereas at the national and even state levels, there is evidence that the media do have considerable discretion to set agendas, this is less true at the local level where journalists and sources are more likely to interact every day in an ongoing relationship.

When the agenda for one city council, determined from the minutes taken during the year, was compared with local newspaper reports of that city council's actions, there was a strong correspondence between the agenda of the council and the subsequent newspaper agenda.[13] But on nearly one third of the topics, the newspaper's ranking differed substantially from the council's, suggesting that independent news judgments were made about the relative importance of these topics. The city council agenda items most likely to be closely reflected on the newspaper agenda were policy matters involving political disputes over how to spend city funds, whereas those council items most likely to be downplayed by the newspaper were administrative matters, such as animal protection, honors and awards, and historical documents. The reporter who covered the city council during the year of the study said that he consciously "boiled down" the more administrative subjects because they were not controversial and did not lend themselves to a story, but tended to be more technical.

Even in covering an important local governing body, reporters do have some discretion about what to emphasize and what to downplay, although this discretion seems to be less than at the national or state level. The reporter interviewed for this study preferred the term *filtering* more than *agenda setting*, because he felt that the agenda-setting label implied the newspaper was creating issues.

INFLUENCING THE MEDIA AGENDA

In addition to political news sources and government public relations, other possible influences on the media agenda include candidate advertising during political campaigns, interest group press releases and conferences, studies reported in specialized journals and publications, poll reports (sometimes initiated by the news media themselves), corporate public relations and dramatic real-world events, not to mention the interests and values of individual journalists themselves.

An increasingly important influence on the media agenda, and thus indirectly on the public agenda, is the work of various interest groups—not only to raise the salience of certain issues, but also to gain attention in the media for facts that support their side of an issue controversy. When the

---

[13]Weaver, D., & Elliott, S. N. (1985). Who sets the agenda for the media? A study of local agenda-building. *Journalism Quarterly, 62,* 87–94.

media ignore such efforts, wealthier interest groups sometimes resort to paid advertising to reach the public. Other times, to get their information to the public, interest groups sponsor research or try to highlight studies by academics and others. Ralph Nader, for example, has been particularly effective in commissioning studies to document his point of view. One of the most prominent was *The Nader Report on the Federal Trade Commission*, a very detailed analysis of that agency's shortcomings in protecting consumers that became a major factor in FTC reform efforts.[14]

Another example of a less extensive study was done by the Children's Defense Fund in 1983 after Congress made changes in the Medicaid program at the request of the Reagan administration. This interest group's report estimated that 700,000 children had lost coverage under the cuts and concluded that "Reaganomics is bad for children's health."[15] This conclusion was quoted in a *New York Times* story about the decline in health services.

Interest groups cannot simply rely on their own distribution of reports to policymakers and opinion leaders. The success of their efforts also depends on how much news coverage they can get.

Another strategy for gaining news coverage, and thus influence on both the media and public agenda, is to make the information easily available at low cost.

> Sources enter into an exchange of value with journalists in which (1) they reduce the costs of news work to increase their control over news content; (2) they reduce the costs of scientific research to increase their control over scientific and technical information; and (3) they even reduce the costs of writing and producing television fiction to increase their control over the cultural background against which social policy questions are generally framed. (p. 15)[16]

Still another way in which interest groups attempt to influence the public agenda is to initiate a public relations campaign, especially if they feel that the press is not devoting enough coverage to their issue or to their point of view. But such campaigns can be very expensive and too short-lived to have much influence on the media, and the public, agenda. Most media agenda-setting studies find that for an issue to become very salient to large numbers of the public, it must receive sustained news coverage over a number of weeks.

---

[14]This example was taken from Berry, op. cit., (p. 143). See also Cox, E. F., Fellmeth, R. C., & Schulz, J. E. (1969). *The Nader report on the federal trade commission.* New York: Baron.

[15]Pear, R., (1983, January 17). Decline in health services for the poor is cited. *The New York Times*, quoted in Berry, op. cit., p. 144.

[16]Gandy, O. H., Jr. (1982). *Beyond agenda-setting: Information subsidies and public policy.* Norwood, NJ: Ablex.

Political demonstrations also are used to directly influence both the policy agenda and the media agenda. As Jeffrey Berry put it, "The first and foremost goal of all political protests is the same: to gain coverage by the media. Like a tree falling in the forest, a protest without media coverage goes unappreciated no matter how much noise it makes" (p. 147).[17] Although protests are often effective in elevating issues on the media agenda, Berry pointed out that protests are rarely convincing enough in themselves not to require other tactics. And he argued that protests have become so common that they are less effective in attracting media coverage than they were in the early days of the civil rights movement in the 1960s.

Interest groups also may have some influence on the media agenda by organizing letter-writing campaigns. There is some evidence that a large number of letters to the editor can influence the amount of subsequent news coverage of an issue.

And, finally, the media agenda is sometimes influenced by what more specialized and professional publications, such as *The New England Journal of Medicine*, are emphasizing. In a book about how child abuse became an important issue, Barbara Nelson found that "the mass media carefully and consistently monitor professional and scientific journals in search of new stories," and that "this symbiotic relationship is perhaps the most neglected factor contributing to ongoing media coverage of issues" (p. 57).[18] She cited a 1962 article, "The Battered Child Syndrome," in the *Journal of the American Medical Association*, as causing a storm in medical circles and in the mass media as well. She also credits this article with providing a powerful, unifying label, "the battered child syndrome," for the issue, and argued that the routine issuing of press releases about important findings such as this by the American Medical Association keeps journalists abreast of medical issues.

Within a week of the news release based on this article in the *AMA Journal, Time* and *Newsweek* magazines reported the findings, followed by reports in *Life* and the *Saturday Evening Post*. Nelson argued that these articles "can be considered the point at which an invisible problem became a public concern, and soon a major public policy issue" (p. 61).[19] Popular magazines publicized the problem in 124 articles published from 1960 through 1980, which Nelson attributed to more than 1,700 articles on child abuse or related subjects appearing in professional journals over the past 30 years. Her findings dramatically support Lippmann's observation that the press "can normally record only what has been recorded for it by the

---

[17]Berry, op. cit., p. 147.

[18]Nelson, B. J. (1984). *Making an issue of child abuse: Political agenda setting for social problems.* Chicago: University of Chicago Press.

[19]Nelson, op. cit., p. 61.

working of institutions," and is therefore "no substitute for institutions" (pp. 361 & 364).[20]

In other words, the media do not set their agendas independently of what other institutions and groups in society are saying and doing, although there is considerable discretion for the media to give more or less emphasis to certain agenda items.

DETERMINING PUBLIC OPINION

Even though many government officials realize that the media often are not valid indicators of public opinion, the media do provide a much quicker indication of the most salient issues of the day than do carefully constructed opinion polls or the systematic analyses of letters and phone calls. And the issues emphasized by the media over time often become more salient to many citizens and voters—a kind of self-fulfilling prophecy that cannot be ignored by most politicians. But there are other ways of influencing policy agendas besides first changing media agendas.

These range from private meetings between lobbyists and legislators to targeted mailings. Although it is often assumed that most interest groups want to reach as many people as possible, Berry pointed out that this is frequently not practical and that many interest groups seek instead to influence the "attentive public," those groups concentrating on particular issues, to prove to government decision makers that these issues are important enough to require government action. Some interest groups bypass the media completely with direct mail campaigns to members of attentive publics, often including voting scorecards or ratings so that these persons will know how their elected representatives have voted on specific issues. Dozens of interest groups now use voting scorecards, including the Americans for Democratic Action (ADA), the Americans for Constitutional Action (ACA), the National Farmers Union, Common Cause, the National Taxpayers Union, and the National Council of Senior Citizens.

But few interest groups rely solely on indirectly influencing policy agendas. Most groups want to build on indirect lobbying by direct contact with policymakers, especially when bills are being debated or agencies are about to write new regulations directly affecting their issues. Direct contacts with policymakers include letter-writing campaigns, telephone calls, and personal visits by interest group members as well as visits by lobbyists themselves. For lobbyists the letters and phone calls of group members are a way of legitimating their activities. When letters and phone calls are coming

---

[20]Lippmann, W. (1922). *Public opinion*. New York: Macmillan.

into a congressman's office, the status of lobbyists is enhanced and their access is likely to be greater than normal.

The key assumption of these efforts is that letters influence government policymakers about both the salience of an issue and what position to take. There is evidence to support this assumption. Members of Congress do keep track of the mail, even though they cannot read every letter. Their staffs summarize and tabulate the sentiments in the letters because the opinions of constituents affect chances for reelection and because most elected officials want to know what the people in their districts think.

When the stakes are particularly high, lobbyists often have important people in their groups come to Washington to meet personally with policymakers. Berry quoted an aircraft industry lobbyist for McDonnell Douglas as saying, there's "no one better to talk about the F-18 fighter than the director [of the company]" (p. 153).[21] Another example concerns the American Newspaper Publishers Association (ANPA) desire to keep American Telephone & Telegraph (AT&T) from publishing information electronically over its telephone lines. The ANPA appealed to local newspaper publishers to lobby their members of Congress, and one House of Representatives aide is reported to have said, "You don't pick a fight with a man who buys his ink by the barrel" (p. 154).[22]

An increase in the number of interest groups has heightened competition among them and competition for access to the policy agendas of various branches of government. Any system of government can process only a small number of demands within any given time period. The agendas of the various branches of government must be limited to a manageable number of issues. Because of this political reality, more attention than ever is being paid to how some issues and interests are successfully transferred onto policy agendas.

CONCLUSIONS

This chapter has explored the complex transfer of interests between private, media, public, and policy agendas in the United States. It should be obvious that even though the media play a more important role in the transfer of interests now than early in this century when Lippmann wrote his influential book, *Public Opinion*, the agenda-setting influence of the media with regard to both public and policy agendas is not unlimited. There are many politicians, lobbyists, public relations specialists, and other news sources who

---

[21]Berry, op. cit., p. 153.

[22]Warner, M. G. (1982, July 9). Newspaper publishers lobby to keep AT&T from role they covet. *Wall Street Journal*, quoted in Berry, op. cit., 154.

are adroit at setting the media agenda as well as responding to it.[23]

The proliferation of interest groups in recent years has made both public and policy agenda setting more complicated and more competitive than in previous times. Coupled with the decline in political party influence and affiliation, these developments have elevated the importance of the news media. Public agenda setting is related to public opinion because what we think about forms a basis for what we think. The manipulation and the consequences of public opinion also have consequences for government policies and allocations of scarce resources.

> Once shaped by the media agenda, the public agenda, may in turn influence the policy agenda of elite decision makers, and, in some cases, policy implementation. Of course in some instances, the media agenda seems to have direct, sometimes strong, influence upon the policy agenda of elite decision makers, and, in some cases, policy implementation. (p. 579)[24]

Because of the limitations of journalism and mass communication noted in earlier chapters, the growing importance of the media in agenda building and agenda setting is not necessarily healthy for democracy. Few journalists are elected by or directly accountable to the public, although most try hard not to be the captives of various special interests and to be as fair and impartial as possible.

James Madison in *The Federalist* No. 10 recognized that factions, or special interests, were sure to form in any open political system and to pursue their own selfish interests, thus posing a danger of oppressing other groups in society.[25] Madison argued that the solution was not to prohibit the right to organize factions, but rather to construct the system in such a way that no one faction could come to dominate others. Political parties were important arbiters of the power and interests of various factions in earlier times, but their influence has declined in the past two decades and has been replaced to some extent by the news media.

While the news media are indeed no substitute for institutions, they are much larger, richer, and more powerful institutions at the end of the 20th century than they were in Lippmann's day. Because of their enhanced status and influence in public and policy agenda setting and in the formation of public opinion, the news media need to redouble their efforts to represent a variety of interests in the society and to make the news agenda more systematically representative of those interests. The mass media remain one of the most influential actors in defining public and policy agendas, and thus the national will.

---

[23]Smith, H. (198). *The power game.* New York: Random House.

[24]Rogers & Dearing, op. cit.

[25]*The federalist papers*, No. 77–84.

Author Index

104

Subject Index